Praise for Replanted

"Jesus often drew vivid word pictures from agriculture—wheat fields and mustard seeds, fig trees and grapevines—to help us see His kingdom, ourselves, and what we most need. *Replanted* does the same, using rich images from the plant world in ways both poetic and practical to help us grasp and feel God's good purposes for us as adoptive and foster families."

—JEDD MEDEFIND, president, Christian Alliance for Orphans

"The loving care of orphans and foster children is the most sacred thing in the world. Those who take on this courageous journey know that it is the greatest of life's joys—but also full of hardships and challenges. With their ministry, the authors of this amazing book have empowered the church to support families with 'replanted' children. They are the most qualified people I know to speak truth into this experience. For both the heroes engaged in adoption or foster care and those of us eager to support them, this book is a must-read."

—DR. WESS STAFFORD, president emeritus, Compassion International, author of *Too Small to Ignore* and *Just a Minute*

"The wall. That is exactly what foster and adoptive parents hit when expectations of the journey collide with the realities of the experience. Authors Jenn, Josh, and Mike understand this experience well and have written an amazing, much needed resource for parents and churches. The analogy of what families need—soil (emotional support), sunlight (informational support), and water (tangible support)—truly speaks to the heart of the need. The exercises at the end of each chapter allow for every reader to build self-awareness, parenting awareness, and God awareness. I highly recommend this book for foster and adoptive parents and the ministries and organizations that support them."

—JAYNE SCHOOLER, author of *Wounded Children, Healing Homes* and *Telling the Truth to Adopted and Foster Children*

"*Replanted* openly explores the challenges faced by children impacted by early trauma believing that hope and healing can come as parents gain the support they need, as support systems become trauma-competent, and as churches become more intentional in the ways they come alongside families built through adoption and foster care. *Replanted* is a timely resource and encouragement for anyone, anywhere, on the journey of adoption and foster care."

—TERRI COLEY, coordinator of
Pre+Post Adoption Support, Show Hope

"*Replanted* provides wise counsel and guidance to those who welcome vulnerable children into their hearts and homes. This resource will challenge and equip, comfort and encourage those on God's journey to love children from hard places, and inform the church about the crucial role it can play in supporting them."

—SHAREN FORD, director of Foster Care & Adoption
Advocacy for Children, Focus on the Family

"Jenn, Josh, and Mike have created something amazing here. Real, authentic conversation about the challenges of this journey combined with hope-filled stories and practical resources that breathe fresh wind in the sails of caregivers. Every foster and adoptive parent will want to have this book on their kitchen table!"

—MICHELE SCHNEIDLER, cofounder of the Refresh Conference
and senior vice president of programs/partnerships
for the 1MILLIONHOME campaign

"We have been waiting for this book that, through personal stories, discussion questions, and the Replanted model of support, brings relevant and fresh solutions to the long-recognized core issues in relinquishment and adoption. Offering hope and tools to this generation of adoptive and foster parents, it also provides the insights needed by members of the Church to extend grace and support to these families."

—REBECCA MacDOUGALL, LCSW, adoptive mother and executive branch director, Bethany Christian Services of Illinois

"As a foster/adoptive parent this book would have saved me years of research and heartache. Not only do Jenn, Josh, and Mike do a fantastic job of taking all different types of research and condensing it down to what is applicable to caregivers, but they do it in a way that is engaging, full of stories, hope, laughter, and tears. They are honest about the deep paradox that exists for families and communities caring for children from trauma. They give practical advice and tools to organizations wanting to support and aid in the healing process, and they do it all with grace and faith. I couldn't recommend this book more; potential caregivers, you need this! Support systems, they need you to know this!"

—AMANDA PURVIS, TBRI training specialist, Karyn Purvis Institute of Child Development

"*Replanted* is a must-have resource for your library! Whether you are an adoptive or foster parent, or you desire to support the ones serving in the trenches, this book is for you. Jenn writes with humility and wisdom from her years of experience working with families. *Replanted* is not a 'roses and butterflies' type of book; it is honest and real and full of hope and practical help to bring healing to your family."   —JAMI KAEB, founder & executive director, The Forgotten Initiative

REPLANTED

Replanted

Faith-Based Support for Adoptive and Foster Families

Jenn Ranter Hook, Joshua N. Hook,
and Mike Berry

TEMPLETON PRESS

Templeton Press
300 Conshohocken State Road, Suite 500
West Conshohocken, PA 19428
www.templetonpress.org

Set in Adobe Caslon Pro by Gopa and Ted2, Inc.

Library of Congress Control Number: 2019930745
ISBN: 978-1-59947-537-0 (pbk: alk. paper)

This paper meets the requirements of ANSI/NISO Z39.48-1992
(Permanence of Paper).

A catalogue record for this book is available from the Library of Congress.

19 20 21 22 23   10 9 8 7 6 5 4 3 2 1

Printed in the United States of America.

To the Replanted leadership team in Chicago, who pioneered and helped breathe life and vision into this ministry—this book is a reflection and extension of what you helped to create.

To my parents, Fred and Laurie; my brother, Craig; and my sister-in-law, Vicki, who have been my biggest cheerleaders in life.

And finally, to my husband, who encouraged me to write this book.

—Jenn Ranter Hook

To my wife, Jenn—I love you and am proud of you!

—Joshua N. Hook

To the amazing, beautiful people who are our support community: there's no way we could do this journey without you!

—Mike Berry

Contents

Preface

ADOPTION AND foster care are holy but difficult work. Parenting children from hard places is one of the most rewarding, meaningful journeys in which you can ever engage. But it is also challenging and stressful. Sometimes adoptive and foster families are struggling and feel overwhelmed, not sure whether they can face tomorrow. As a therapist who worked in the foster care system, and later as a leader of a ministry serving adoptive and foster families, I saw the joys and challenges of adoptive and foster parenting first-hand. I saw the meaning and the struggles, the beauty and the pain.

One of the things I realized was that adoptive and foster families needed more support. I walked alongside many children in foster care who had been abused and neglected, who were often misunderstood as misbehaved or problematic children rather than being seen as precious and worthy with a complex history that had shaped their present reality. As a Christian, I sat through sermons where the preacher would talk about how Christians should prioritize orphan care or encourage members of the congregation to adopt and foster. At the same time, however, I noticed that church after church provided almost zero help and support after a family adopted or fostered. Something was missing here. I knew there was an awesome opportunity for Christians and the church to help support adoptive and foster families who were struggling, but we were missing it—and families were paying the price.

That's why I wrote *Replanted: Faith-Based Support for Adoptive and Foster Families*. If you're an adoptive or foster family, or thinking about being one, I want to be honest about the joys and difficulties of the journey. I want you to enter your adoptive and foster experience with eyes wide open. I don't do this to scare you; instead, I want you to be prepared for the challenges along the way. Specifically, I want to encourage you to get the help and support you need to thrive.

Maybe you're not an adoptive or foster family, but you have a close family member or friend who has adopted or fostered, and you want to help. This book is for you as well. I want you to be informed about the needs of adoptive and foster families so that you can help in a way that is balanced and effective. Too often people are misinformed, and they try to help in a manner that actually does more harm than good. I want you to be an effective helper.

Finally, maybe you work at a church and you want your church to be a safe and supportive place for adoptive and foster families. You see families in your congregation who are struggling, but you don't know how best to help. This book is for you too. One of my dreams is for churches to partner together to resource ministries to effectively support adoptive and foster families. This book gives you the tools for how to do that as well.

Wherever you are, thanks for taking this journey with me. I'd also like to invite God along with us. I firmly believe that God places a high priority on caring for vulnerable children, and we are all called to be a part of the mission and work he is doing. Some amazing things are happening in the world of caring for vulnerable children, and it's exciting to partner with God on that road together. I'm glad you're here.

Jenn Ranter Hook

Acknowledgments

IN 2011, I was introduced to a pastor named Gregory Whittaker at a farewell party for a friend. After learning that I worked as a therapist in foster care, he asked what seemed like a simple question: "What do you see as the church's role in supporting our families?" Gregory, I bet you had no idea what you were getting yourself into, but thanks for believing in me and advocating for our church to actively love and serve our adoptive and foster community. Replanted exists because of you. Church of the Resurrection, thanks for saying "yes" and for faithfully praying for and supporting our adoptive and foster care community.

I want to give a huge shout out to my original team in Chicago that helped pioneer and breathe life into the Replanted Ministry at its inception. Scott and Sarah Roney, Mike Swihart, Christie Otts, and Michelle Peterson: Your dedication, passion, and vision to support the families in our community through the local church has brought us to where we are today.

Our team of dedicated leaders and volunteers has consistently shown up and served as the hands and feet of Jesus to our families. You are the heartbeat of this ministry. Thank you for all the ways you lead and love our families, from launching groups, attending meetings, setting up tables and chairs, playing with and investing in the kids, and faithfully praying for, sitting with, and listening to the hearts of our parents. There are so many people to thank for their dedication, leadership, and service: Hollee Ball, Currey and JJ Blandford, Melissa Harms, Mark Hawkinson, Lisa Jarot, Laura

Leonard, Sonja Shogren, Christine Stahl, Jessica Stoffer, David Vosburg, Chris Wilson, and David Wrigglesworth. You are true rock stars.

To the Replanted leadership, group facilitators, hosts, and mentors around the country: It's been an honor to share this passion and calling in life with you. Thank you for dedicating your lives to sit with our families in both the joy and the pain, mentoring and investing in the lives of our children, and being kingdom influencers.

To all the children that forever changed my life while I worked at the Youth Service Bureau: This ministry was created for you. Thank you for trusting me with your hearts and your stories.

To all the Replanted families we've had the privilege of supporting and journeying with: Thank you for your faithfulness in this journey, even when it's hard. It brings us great joy to do life together, to hold one another's arms up when we feel weary, and to celebrate the joys with fierce abandon. We love you dearly and are cheering so hard for you and your precious kiddos.

To Mike and Kristin, Andrew and Michelle, and Jami K: Thanks for being kindred spirits in ministry. It's been quite the ride, and I'm grateful for your support and partnership.

To Susan and the team at Templeton Press: Thank you for believing in this book and taking a chance on us. We are so grateful for your support.

I want to give a huge thanks to my mentors. Patmarie Hawkinson, thanks for intentionally investing in my life, letting me share vulnerably, and being my champion. I'm forever grateful for your guidance, prayer, hospitality, and countless hours around the campfire. Karen Miller, thanks for being my leadership coach. Your encouragement, wisdom, and guidance has been so valuable and helped shape who I am today.

To my high school teachers and coaches Mr. Buma and Mr. Roukema: My course in life was altered because of you. Thank you for challenging me to be my best, believing in me when I didn't believe in myself, seeing what I couldn't see, coaching me, and cheering for me. Thanks for seeing the real me. I am where I am today because of you.

To my friends who are more like family in Canada and Wheaton: Thanks for doing life with me. You have taught me the value of deep, genuine, grace-filled relationships. To Karen, Paige, and my 868 girls, I love you! To Brenda and Randy, thanks for being like second parents to me and encouraging my competitive nature. To Aunt Trish, my hockey aunt, you are simply the best!

To my crazy, ridiculous, goofball family: Who would have thought a dairy farmer's daughter would write a book someday! "Ranter" is on this book as a reflection of the impact you have had on my life. I miss you all the time. Mom and Dad, you always knew God had big plans for my life. Thanks for supporting that, even though it has led me far away from doing life with you. Craig, little broski, you have taught me so much! Thanks for being my friend and for fiercely protecting me.

And finally, to my husband, Josh Hook, who encouraged me to write this book. I seriously would never have done this without your support. When we first met, I was terrified to let you read anything I wrote. Look how far we've come. I'm so blessed to be married to you. Thanks for so fiercely believing in me. You were worth the wait.

—Jenn Ranter Hook

SECTION 1

Introduction and Theoretical Foundation

CHAPTER I

Caring for Vulnerable Children
Is Challenging *and* Beautiful

The beginning is always today.
—MARY WOLLSTONECRAFT

As I (Jenn) begin to write this book, my mind wanders back to one of our Parents' Night Out events, which is an event our ministry organizes so that adoptive and foster parents can have a night out to themselves and our kiddos can build relationships with one another. We get a group of volunteers together and come up with a bunch of fun activities for the children so that the parents can get a few hours to go out alone. One husband told me that he and his wife were planning to have dinner at the local Olive Garden, and we laughed, agreeing on our mutual love for the unlimited salad and breadsticks. Another couple was planning to see a movie with a few friends. They hadn't been out to see a movie in—well, they couldn't remember the last time. Another couple hadn't planned anything. They chuckled and said that maybe they would just go home and take a nap. I wasn't sure if they were joking or not. But one thing was clear, our parents needed this time to recharge and care for themselves, and for some, our offering of Parents' Night Out was the only opportunity they would get.

We had a great time with the kids. It was fun to see the children laughing, playing, and connecting with one another. As I ventured from room to room, I realized we were also creating a deeper community for our kids—where they could be with others on a similar journey and know that they are not alone. The night went off without any major problems or incidents. Sure, there was a bathroom accident, but luckily the parents had left a change of underwear and clothes. I had to intervene in a few places where the children were having a tough time, and the volunteers weren't sure what to do. I chuckle, remembering my then-boyfriend Josh (who is now my husband) struggling to problem-solve with a young girl who didn't want to be in the group she was assigned to, but who started to cry and scream when Josh suggested she join a different group because her bracelet didn't match the new group's. When the children arrived, they were each given a colored bracelet to help them remember which team leader they were with for the evening. Her bracelet was orange, but the group she wanted to be in had purple. Josh quickly dug through the materials and found an extra bracelet that matched the color of the new group and calmed the crisis. Many readers can likely understand the difficulty our children can experience with transitions like this one.

As the night came to a close and the parents came by to pick up their children, I reflected on what had happened. Although the evening was energizing, and I loved the ministry and playing with the kids, I was tired. It was a lot of work, and I was ready to head home and go to sleep. Something clicked, and I realized I recognized a similar feeling reflected in each of the parents' eyes who dropped off their kids that night. They were tired. Being an adoptive and foster parent was energizing and rewarding, but it was also draining. Their lives were filled with joy and love for their children, as well as the satisfaction of joining with God to engage in the meaningful pursuit of caring for the vulnerable. But responding to the trauma and special needs that are unique to children impacted by adoption or foster care is challenging.

The paradox here is that the journey is beautiful and difficult all at the same time. As a former therapist for children in foster care, and then as a leader of a ministry for adoptive and foster families,

I had the privilege of coming in and out of the lives of families and (hopefully) offering some support, help, and hope. But the parents and families were the real shepherds. These were the people who were giving it their all, day after day, even when they felt they had nothing left to give. I smiled, recognizing that we all had an important part to play in responding to God's call to care for vulnerable children, and this was holy work, kingdom work. Then I packed up and went home to bed.

The journey of adoption and foster care is rewarding and meaningful. Many adoptive and foster parents say their parenting journey is the most meaningful and joyful part of their lives. I remember one adoptive mom who teared up when she was reflecting. Even though her two adopted girls had gone through some tough times, she said, "I wouldn't trade in my family for anything. They are my world." Caring for vulnerable children is deeply connected with the heart of God. Opening up your home and family to a child in need is incredibly moving and amazing. Adoption and foster care connect with important values that are deeply integral to what it means to be a Christian. It is a beautiful expression of *love*: it involves caring and sacrifice for a child in need. It is a powerful expression of *justice*: it involves meeting the needs of vulnerable children and the "least of these." And it is a wonderful expression of *faithfulness*: it involves sticking with a child for the long haul, whether that is permanently or temporarily, and through the inevitable ups and downs. Being willing to serve as an adoptive or foster parent involves becoming the hands and feet of Jesus to a child. If you are involved on this journey, you are doing a great and mighty thing. I am in awe of your love, commitment, and faithfulness.

But another reality is just as true: being an adoptive parent, foster parent, or kinship caregiver (i.e., a relative, such as a grandparent, who cares for the child when the child's biological parents are unable to do so) can be challenging. If you are on this journey right now, you know this in a unique and personal way. The challenges can feel overwhelming and might leave you feeling alone, rejected, and isolated. You might even question whether you should have become an adoptive or foster parent in the first place.

These struggles are a reality for many of our adoptive and foster families, but there is also hope. Hope for things to get better. Hope for healing and growth, both for you as a parent, your children, and your family. Hope for you and your family to get support—to get your needs met in a real, tangible way. Hope for God to be alive and moving in the midst of your pain and struggle. The hope we speak of may not mean that everything is working out, your children are behaving, your home is peaceful, or all of your plans are lining up the way you thought they would. Sometimes hope is found in the middle of the dark or defeating circumstances in which we find ourselves. It is in knowing and trusting that your Heavenly Father is holding on to you, even when the storms in your life are the fiercest, and that he willingly steps into our mess. Hope is also found when we join with others who are on the journey. We'll talk more about support later, but it's important to note here that hope is found through Jesus, and that often comes to life more than anything through our relationship with others who are on this journey with us.

WHO THIS BOOK IS FOR

Where are you in your journey of adoption and foster care? Throughout this book, I use the phrase "adoption and foster care," but this book is for anyone involved in caring for vulnerable children—including adoptive parents, foster parents, kinship caregivers, Safe Families parents, and those who are considering such type of involvement. (Safe Families is an organization that provides temporary respite care for children whose parents need additional support, without having their child removed and placed in a foster home. Parents maintain guardianship of their child and have access to their child while the child stays with a Safe Family. Placements can range anywhere from one day to one year in length, and it is completely voluntary on the parents' part. For example, a mother who is having surgery may not have anyone to care for her children while she is recovering, so she can place her children with a Safe Family until she is back on her feet again.)

Maybe you are at the beginning of your journey. Maybe you feel a call to care for vulnerable children but you don't know exactly what that looks like yet. Or maybe you are in the middle of your journey and are having a tough time. You recognize the beauty of the journey but are also having difficulties and need support. Or maybe you don't personally feel called to adopt or foster, but you still feel a strong call to do something. It may be a realization that the folks in your congregation or neighborhood are struggling and could use a helping hand. You want to support adoptive and foster families, but you don't know how to best do that. Or perhaps you have friends or family who have adopted or fostered, and you are struggling to walk alongside them in the journey and understand why adoptive or foster parenting is unique compared to more traditional types of parenting.

Wherever you are in your journey, this book is a guide for you. Many adoptive and foster families are struggling and feel as if they are alone. At a foundational level, the heart of this book is for you to feel validated and supported right where you are—in the beauty and the struggle. The reality is that the adoption and foster care journey involves joy and heartache—death and resurrection. I long for you to know, at a deep, heart level, that you are not alone. We all need safe, loving, grace-filled relationships and communities that accept our families right where we are—in our beautiful messes.

I hope this book encourages you and lets you know that you are not alone, and you are not crazy. Also, I want to acknowledge that sometimes friends, family, and the church can have good intentions and try to help, but this "help" can actually do more harm than good. For example, maybe your church told you it couldn't meet the needs of your child, so your child couldn't come to Sunday school anymore. Maybe you had a friend who immediately tried to give you advice when you were struggling, even though she didn't understand your situation or your child. If you have been hurt during this journey by your friends, family, or church community, I am deeply sorry. It might feel difficult to get into a place where you feel safe to reach out for help again. That makes sense.

Throughout this book, you will read stories of adoptive and foster families who are just like you—facing real-life challenges and doing the rewarding but sometimes exhausting work of parenting children from hard places. I try to be honest with these stories. I don't shy away from the pain and struggle, but I also want to share stories of families working through their difficult circumstances and recognizing that they are not alone. You will also learn about the importance of support—what kinds of support systems exist for adoptive and foster families, and how you can advocate for yourself and your family to get the support you need. You will also learn about how churches can work to support adoptive and foster families and invite these families to participate fully in the richness of a loving, grace-filled community.

In the end, my goal is that you will be instilled with hope, wherever you are—not hope that your problems will go away or that you will suddenly solve all your children's difficulties and problems. Although great, that would be impossible. I can't remove or take away your difficulty and struggle. Instead, my goal is that you will experience hope and understand that it is possible to experience a full, vibrant, healthy life as an adoptive and foster family. You can learn new skills to help you improve your relationship with your child and with your spouse. You can gather a group of faithful people around you to help support you through your ups and downs. You can have people who understand you and have your back, no matter what. And you can be a church community that actively cares for vulnerable children and supports adoptive and foster families in a way that really works.

OUR STORIES

Let me tell you a bit about myself and my background. My name is Jenn Ranter Hook. I'm originally from Canada, and I moved to the United States to attend graduate school at Wheaton College, which is near Chicago. After getting my master's in clinical psychology, I worked as a therapist in the foster care system. In my work with children and families, I first recognized that families needed more support.

For example, I remember working with Lindsey (age five) and Edward (age eight). These siblings had been placed in a Christian foster home, and I started doing therapy with each of the children, and occasionally the parents as well. The parents were loving and supportive and had a genuine heart to care for vulnerable children. They felt a call from God to foster and prayerfully considered this call for some time before committing to the journey. They also had two other children in the home (two boys—one three years old and another eighteen months).

Even though they were in a good place as a family, the parents were in deep trenches with Lindsey and Edward. The siblings were experiencing some serious emotional and behavioral problems at the time of their placement. Lindsey had been sexually abused, which was the primary reason for the children going into foster care in the first place. She would act out, escalating from zero to a hundred in the blink of an eye. The parents also once found Lindsey playing doctor with their three-year-old son and were uncertain about whether this was developmentally normative or might represent a repetition of her previous sexual abuse. Edward was struggling as well, especially with feelings of sadness and depression. He also didn't want to leave his biological parents and seemed down and withdrawn most days. At one point, the foster parents came into therapy because Edward had tried to run away on multiple occasions, and had also tried to cut himself with a knife. At age eight, Edward told them that he wanted to kill himself, and they just didn't know how to handle that. He was troubled that he was not able to protect his sister from the abuse she experienced, and he desperately wanted to return home to his mother.

As I sat with the parents in the therapy room, we worked through several issues. We talked about the effects of trauma on children, and I normalized the reactions Lindsey and Edward were having. We discussed the need to adapt parenting strategies to help children who have trauma histories. We came up with a plan for keeping Lindsey, Edward, and their children safe. And throughout the course of therapy, Lindsey and Edward made progress. Lindsey was able to share her feelings with me, and later with her foster and birth parents, which helped reduce her acting-out behaviors. She learned coping skills for how to take care of herself when she started to escalate. Edward was able to communicate some of his sadness through play therapy, and he no longer was suicidal. There were bright spots as a family—movie nights, play dates in the park, and soccer games.

We also spent a lot of time talking about support. As with many families I saw, the parents were more or less on their own. They didn't have adequate support from their friends, family, or church community. Their children felt alone. They felt alone, as if they were the only ones struggling with these kinds of issues. As a therapist, I knew other families living with similar kinds of issues and feelings. The aloneness these families felt was destroying any hope the families had for healing and growth. I couldn't help but think, *Where is the church in this?*

From this place a group of us developed an organization called Replanted (www.ReplantedMinistry.org) in 2011, a ministry that organizes and provides faith-based support for adoptive and foster families. Replanted is a place for families wherever they are on their journey. Parents are encouraged to get involved with support from the very beginning, even as they are working to discern their call from God to foster or adopt. The vast majority of our parents are in the trenches, working day to day in both the beauty and the struggle that is adoptive and foster parenting. We help facilitate authentic community with others who understand the joy as well as the challenge and struggle of adoption and foster care. I remember one adoptive parent who approached me in disbelief about the support she received from participating in a Replanted group with others who truly got it. She had a strong support network of friends in her area, but none who understood the adoption or foster care journey firsthand. The support she received from others speaking a similar language was unlike anything she had experienced. I remember her saying with tears in her eyes, "This ministry is filling a void of support I didn't realize I needed until now."

Replanted also provides a way for church communities to get involved in a real, tangible way to partner with and support adoptive and foster families. We all have a significant role to play. The call to care for vulnerable children is deeply biblical and something that can unite the church. Replanted is not about one church, but about *the church* as we seek to be the unified body of Christ. This book was born out of my experiences over the years as both a therapist and a leader of a national organization that works to provide support to adoptive and foster families.

It has been especially rewarding to write this book as a team with two coauthors, and this volume also draws on their experiences and expertise. (The book is written from my voice for the ease of reading, but the content reflects our collective experience.) Joshua Hook isn't just my coauthor; he is also my husband, and it has been a blast to dream about and work on this project together. Josh earned his PhD in counseling psychology from Virginia Commonwealth University, and he currently works as a professor at the University of North Texas. He has done quite a bit of research on topics relevant to this book, including humility, forgiveness, healthy relationships and marriage, and Christian counseling. He is also a licensed clinical psychologist in Texas and author of a book on leading small groups (Hook, Hook, & Davis, 2017) that we use to train small group leaders in the Replanted ministry. He also blogs about personal and spiritual growth at www.JoshuaNHook.com. I draw on his research expertise and clinical experience throughout the book.

Then there is my good friend and colleague Mike Berry. Mike and his wife, Kristin, have adopted eight children. In addition to being adoptive parents, Mike and Kristin served as foster parents for eight years. Mike has the firsthand personal experience of what it is like to be in the trenches and feel as if you have little or no support around you. Partly in response to Mike and Kristin's own struggles and needs, Mike has been involved in supporting adoptive and foster families for many years. He is cocreator of the award-winning blog Confessions of an Adoptive Parent, which provides helpful resources for parents, and he also speaks regularly at conferences around the United States on adoptive and foster parenting.

STORIES OF ADOPTIVE AND FOSTER CARE FAMILIES

Throughout this book, I share stories of adoptive and foster families to illustrate key themes and topics of the book. The cases are based on actual experiences with adoptive and foster families, but the names, identifying information, and some details of the stories have been changed to protect confidentiality. I hope these examples help you recognize that you are not alone.

For example, maybe you'll connect with the story of Josie and Michael. Josie and Michael married in their mid-twenties and had a great first few years of marriage, traveling and getting settled in their careers, church, and community. In their late twenties, they decided to start having kids, but it didn't happen right away. After two years of trying, they saw a fertility doctor, which ultimately led to trying in vitro fertilization (IVF), which was unsuccessful. This news was devastating for Josie and Michael, who needed to grieve that they could not have their own biological children.

Still wanting a family of their own, Josie and Michael decided to adopt internationally, and after a long and expensive adoption process, they adopted a two-year-old girl named Sara from Ukraine. Sara had been placed in an orphanage at birth, which was the only home she had known until she was adopted. Sara was a precious little girl who loved playing dress-up and running around outside. She was a curious child, and Josie and Michael loved walking as a family in the forest preserve behind their house. Every tree, flower, or bug was a new adventure. Josie and Michael loved seeing the world through Sara's eyes. Their family felt more complete, as if something missing had been put in its place.

Although adopting Sara was a joyous occasion, parts of the journey were also difficult and painful. The adoption agency didn't have a lot of details about Sara's family history, but there was concern that Sara's mother had used alcohol and drugs while she was pregnant. Sara showed signs of developmental delays, and she had difficulty attaching to Josie and Michael. She would cry when she was left alone, but when Josie or Michael would try to hold and comfort her, Sara struggled to calm down. Sara had a hard time regulating her emotions and would often hit and bite other children. Because of Sara's emotional and behavioral problems, Josie and Michael had trouble asking friends and family to agree to babysit so that they could get some time for self-care. The nursery and Sunday school teachers were kind, but eventually they told Josie and Michael that one of them would have to stay with Sara because of complaints from the other parents about her aggressive behavior. Going to church together as a family became tough. Even Josie's family, who lived in the area and were very supportive at the beginning of the adoption process, began to make excuses for why they couldn't babysit or watch Sara.

After a while, these obstacles began to wear on the young couple. They loved Sara deeply, but they became worn-down, tired, and overwhelmed, and they felt ill-equipped to parent a child with developmental delays. Michael and Josie felt as if they were the only ones advocating for their precious little girl. Furthermore, they felt alone. They had thought they had a good support system in place when they began the adoption process, but as Sara's emotional and behavioral problems became more visible, their support system seemed to melt away before their eyes. Friends and family wouldn't return their calls, and those people who did stick around couldn't relate to Josie and Michael's experience. They didn't understand why Sara was acting the way that she did. Some people would give Josie and Michael advice or criticize the job they were doing as parents. Josie and Michael even began to question themselves. Were they doing something wrong? Were they bad parents? Was there any hope of things getting better?

These challenges were also leading to problems in Josie and Michael's marriage. Because of their struggles with support and babysitting, they hadn't been on an actual date in several months. Parenting was taking a toll on their physical health as well. Neither was sleeping or resting enough. Josie used to be a regular at her Pilates class, and Michael enjoyed playing basketball with the guys each week, but it seemed impossible for them to engage in these activities given their increased levels of stress and Sara's pressing needs. Josie and Michael were arguing more, and they hadn't had sex in three months. Both felt frustrated. Something needed to change, but they didn't see a clear way to do something different.

Or maybe you'll connect with the story of Greg and Kristin. They had two children (Brian, age twelve, and Jenny, age ten). After hearing a sermon at their church on caring for vulnerable children, Greg and Kristin both felt convicted that God wanted them to do something to help meet this need. They felt as if they were in a good place with their family, and after several months of prayer and discernment, they felt that God was leading them to be a foster family. They wanted to provide a loving and safe home for a child in need, while the foster care agency worked toward reunification with the child's birth family.

Soon after going through the process of preparing themselves and their home to be foster parents, they received their first placement: two brothers named David and Jay (ages eight and six). Greg and Kristin, as well as their children, were excited about the new additions to their family. They prepped the boy's bedroom and received donations of clothes, toys, and school supplies from their church. The social worker brought the boys to Greg and Kristin's home two weeks later.

David and Jay presented with moderate levels of emotional and behavioral problems as a result of the trauma they experienced. The brothers had been physically abused by their mother's paramour before a school counselor was made aware of the abuse and reported it. The investigation determined that the boys needed to live with a foster family while their mother worked on being a safe and healthy parent. The boys felt confused about why they couldn't stay with their mother. They thought their mother was awesome and loved her deeply, and added to the trauma they experienced was the trauma of separation from her. Both contributed to their emotional and behavioral difficulties.

When they first arrived in care, the boys asked Greg and Kristin when they would be able to return home to their mother. Greg and Kristin did their best to answer the almost overwhelming number of questions that David and Jay had, but many times the answers were unknown. David tended to externalize his problems and frustrations, yelling at Greg and Kristin whenever they would try to enforce a rule or boundary with him. He would become deregulated for prolonged periods of time, and nothing seemed to help calm him down. Jay, on the other hand, tended to internalize his problems. He didn't act out as much, but he was quiet and would shut down, sometimes not even responding when Greg, Kristin, or the kids would try to reach out and include him in conversations or activities. The boys began weekly counseling to process all their big feelings and work through their trauma experiences.

Greg and Kristin began adjusting, but they quickly realized there were so many ups and downs, unknowns, and big feelings that came along with being foster parents. Among the positive things were that Greg and Kristin felt deeply that they were doing what God wanted them to do. They were providing a safe and loving home for the boys in their time of limbo. There were times when David and Jay seemed genuinely appreciative of Greg and Kristin's efforts. Greg, Brian, David, Jenny, and Jay would sometimes all play basketball together in the front driveway, and their laughing and energy could fill the house with joy.

The unknowns did become overwhelming for the family. Greg and Kristin constantly felt pulled in opposite directions. They wanted the boys to reunify with their mother when it was safe and possible to do so. On the one hand, they developed a relationship with the biological mother, and she was making progress toward her goals. On the other hand, sometimes she would make poor choices or miss a weekly visit. When she missed a visit, the boys would be devastated and upset. They started displaying more and more emotional and behavioral difficulties, which made Greg and Kristin feel upset and protective of the boys. The courthouse, weekly visitations, therapy appointments, social worker visits, school meetings, and frequent phone calls from their foster care agency all became the norm.

Living in this state was hard for everyone. Greg and Kristin were stressed and overwhelmed, but doing their best. They loved caring for David and Jay, but they longed for empathic support. When Greg and Kristin would share their experience with friends and family, some were able to listen nonjudgmentally and offer grace and support. Some were understandably upset as well and gave all sorts of advice. Some encouraged Greg and Kristin to stick it out, while others said enough was enough: it was time to send David and Jay back.

Unfortunately, stories like Greg and Kristin's are all too familiar to the foster and adoptive journey. We are often in an uphill climb with our kids because of their trauma and special circumstances. These are precious kids, but trauma manifests itself in so many ways. The story of Greg and Kristin brings up the need for community for the parents and the children, and that's precisely what we're going to discuss in the coming chapters.

ORGANIZATION AND STRUCTURE OF THE BOOK

This book is organized in three major sections. The first section presents the book's theoretical foundation. In chapter 2, I take an in-depth look at what life in the trenches looks like for adoptive and foster families. I think it is important to present an honest picture of the challenges that many adoptive and foster families face, because it is from this accurate place of the gravity of the needs involved that we try to come up with a workable plan for support. I discuss some of the common challenges facing adoptive and foster parents, such as struggles with infertility, parenting at an older age, and parenting a child from a different cultural background. I also address some of the unique challenges for adoptive and foster children, including a history of trauma, attachment difficulties, and emotional and behavioral problems.

I discuss in chapter 3 the Christian call to care for vulnerable children, as well as those who have been orphaned. First, I explore what I believe to be God's heart toward children who, by definition, are orphans because they have lost their biological parents. At a foundational level, God's heart for children in this state is connected with the core message of Christianity: we are all adopted into God's family as sons and daughters. I then take a deep dive into God's heart for children in these circumstances as illustrated in God's relationship with the Israelites in the Old Testament, the life and teachings of Jesus, and the work of the early church. I also focus on the importance of wisdom and discernment in the Christian call to care for vulnerable children. In addition to encouraging us to think about where God is calling us to get involved, I also encourage entering into this journey with a strong dose of humility, an awareness of our limitations, and appropriate boundaries.

The second section of the book presents the Replanted model of support for adoptive and foster families. I highlight the need for a good support system in place throughout the adoption and foster care journey. Using the metaphor of a child being "replanted" in a new family, in chapter 4 I address emotional support, or the "good soil" necessary for a flourishing adoptive or foster family. It is critical to be in relationship with others who understand the journey—people who can say "me too" when you are experiencing pain, difficulty, struggle, and even small victories. I stress the need to develop relationships and communities characterized by grace, safety, and vulnerability. I also talk about practical steps that adoptive and foster parents can take to initiate and seek out these relationships to get the support they need.

As a follow-up to discussing emotional support, I focus in chapter 5 on informational support, or the "sunlight" necessary for thriving as an adoptive and foster parent. Children impacted by the loss of their first family often come from difficult places. Many have experienced trauma and have complex histories. Many do not respond well to traditional parenting discipline practices such as enforcing consequences and removal of privileges. However, adoptive and foster parents are not generally given the necessary training and education to bring their child to a place of healing. As a result, some parents find their child's behavior perplexing, confusing, and even frustrating. I'll cover some of the key issues related to parenting through adoption or foster care, and also discuss some key strategies for getting additional information, education, and support.

Tangible support, or the "water" needed for thriving adoptive and foster families, is my topic in chapter 6. Sometimes adoptive and foster parents struggle with getting basic needs met for their children, such as therapeutic services, school supports (e.g., Individualized Education Programs [IEPs]), and medical care. Foster parents may find it especially frustrating to advocate for their child's needs with the state. If friends and family initially were supportive in regard to tangible needs such as child care, these support systems can dissolve quickly as the support system begins to get a clear understanding of the needs and associated difficulties of the child. Often people have a lot of energy to help and provide support at the beginning of the adoption or foster care journey, but this can wane as the excitement of a new child begins to wear off. I discuss avenues and strategies for obtaining tangible support, as well as some of our psychological blocks with stating clearly the kinds of support we need from others.

The third section of the book explores what support looks like in context. The topic of chapter 7 is support from the perspective of the family member or friend of the adoptive and foster family. Specifically, I talk about how you can help without hurting. I also discuss some of the common pitfalls and ways that people can try to help that actually do more harm than good. Finally, I share resources and ways that anyone can improve one's own training and education in order to be more helpful when supporting adoptive and foster parents and children.

In addition to exploring how we can help support adoptive and foster families at the individual, relational level, I address support at the organization or church level in chapter 8. Churches often put forth that orphan care is an important value, and they want to help support families. However, they may not know how to provide this support in a way that is effective and actually works. Using examples from real churches that have been successful in creating thriving orphan care ministries, I cover some of the key ways that churches can work to provide a sustainable ministry that provides crucial support to adoptive and foster families.

Chapter 9 provides a send-off and encouragement as you continue your journey. In this concluding chapter, I share some of my deepest hopes and dreams for you—specifically that you would feel supported and find community as you continue in this important work of caring for vulnerable children. I believe God calls us all to play a role in such care, but he also wants us to enter this journey in a way that is balanced, wise, and life-giving. Support is the key way to provide the best chance to make that happen.

Moving Forward

I'm so glad you are here with me on this journey. When I sat with families, more than anything I wanted them to feel that they were not alone. I wanted them to know that I was with them, I empathized with their struggle, and I had their back. That's the same desire I have for you. There is incredible, healing hope in understanding this, especially when we are struggling and feeling isolated. Discovering others who have the same limp or the same wounds that we have can be ointment to our souls. While it may not solve the issues you are facing, the discovery does give you strength to face the next day. We're in this together—and it's a good thing we are, because the challenges are significant. We need everyone working together, and we need God, too, if we are to provide those loving, supportive families in which our precious children "will be called oaks of righteousness, a planting of the LORD for the display of his splendor" (Isaiah 61:3b).

EXERCISE: WHERE ARE YOU NOW?

My goal for this book is for you to engage with it as you read. In fact, one of the best ways to process the material is to work through the book with others who are also on this adoption or foster journey. This might be your spouse, but you could also invite others, such as friends, family, and church members. Each chapter closes with some discussion questions to allow you to reflect on and engage with the material.

Reflect on where you are in your journey in adoption and foster care. Maybe you are at the beginning of your journey, trying to discern God's heart for you and your family. Perhaps you are in the middle of the journey, experiencing both the joy and the struggle. You may even be experiencing more of the struggle part of the equation, and you want to figure out how to get back in balance. You might not even feel called to adopt or foster yourself, but you long to support others who are in the trenches.

Where are you in your adoption or foster care journey?

_____

_____

_____

_____

_____

What are some of the main things you hope to learn from reading this book?

_____

_____

_____

_____

_____

What fears do you have in reading this book?

_____

_____

_____

_____

_____

CHAPTER 2

Life in the Trenches

Children are a great comfort in your old age—
and they help you reach it faster too.

—LIONEL KAUFFMAN

IN THESE NEXT two chapters, I want to get real and honest with you about some of the joys and especially some of the challenges that come along with caring for vulnerable children. It's important to enter into this process with your eyes wide open and "count the costs" (Luke 14:28). Some of you have already entered this journey, and my hope is that this information will confirm that you aren't crazy: the stress is real! Also, for those of you who are contemplating the journey, this is an opportunity to consider the specific stressors that can accompany foster and adoptive parenting (chapter 2) as well as the biblical call to not only care for vulnerable children but to discern your decisions with wisdom (chapter 3).

So much joy and meaning come along with being an adoptive or foster parent. The first moments when you meet and wrap your arms around your child are precious. You are providing a child with love, safety, and a family, whether permanently through adoption or temporarily through foster care or Safe Families. This is a deep and holy endeavor. Many of the adoptive and foster families I have had the privilege to work with describe their adoptive or foster journey as the part of their lives that provides them with the deepest source of meaning and purpose.

For example, I remember working in counseling with Janie (age six). Like many children in the foster care system, Janie faced a lot of difficulties and challenges. She had been sexually abused by a member of her extended family, and she struggled with maintaining appropriate boundaries, as well as lashing out in anger toward others. When she became upset, calming her down would sometimes take over an hour. When I first met Janie, she didn't say a word. She had a sweet demeanor about her, but for the first couple of months all she was able to do was climb in my lap and cry for the entire hour. I could only imagine what she had been through that brought her to this place of grief. Slowly, over time, she began talking with me. First we talked about safe and innocent things like school, her favorite toys, and her favorite activities. Then she began reenacting her sexual abuse experiences and expressing her feelings toward others through play therapy. It took months of working through her trauma before I saw joy on her face.

But little by little, Janie did make some progress. The steps were small but important. I made a connection with her, and she began to develop a relationship with me and trust me. Her outbursts of anger slowly decreased, and she was able to participate in a family dinner without melting down. I still remember the first time Janie's mom told me that Janie told her, "I love you." It might seem like a small thing, but for Janie's mom, it was a major breakthrough. Janie eventually had more good than bad days at school. There were definitely still challenges, and the family would get disappointed when setbacks occurred. But there was also hope for Janie to experience healing from her traumatic experiences.

While adoptive and foster families experience joy and hope, the journey can also be hard. There is a deep paradox here: the adoption or foster care journey is at the same time deeply meaningful and deeply challenging. Intense joy and sadness come together. The purpose and meaning are intermingled with pain and struggle. Adoptive mom Jody Landers put it so beautifully: "A child born to another woman calls me 'Mom.' The depth of the tragedy and the magnitude of the privilege are not lost on me."

I remember working with a foster child in therapy who was ultimately not able to reunify with his birth parents because of their continued struggles with drug abuse. The foster family went through the process to adopt him, and joy and excitement were associated with that process. They loved this child and looked forward to adopting him. Likewise, the child I was working with loved his foster family, and this was a good, safe placement for him. I was happy that he would have loving parents and wouldn't spend the next ten years of his life bouncing around in foster homes. Yet he also longed to be reunited with his birth parents, and pain emerged when it became clear that this would not happen. As his adoption day approached, many people in his life had so much joy and anticipation, but he was still grieving and felt like it was hard to match their emotions. For him, that day he would lose hope that he could live with his birth parents again. There was beauty in the adoption process; the boy was replanted into a family who would love him as their own. The beauty, though, was mixed with the grief and loss associated with leaving his birth parents forever.

These mixed emotions are prevalent in adoptive and foster families. Many Christians focus on the positive things about adoption and foster care—and there are many. At the same time, if we only focus on the positives, we neglect the fullness of people's experiences. To truly serve adoptive and foster families, we must honor the entirety of the journey. In this chapter, we take a closer look at some of these stresses and challenges. The purpose isn't to scare you, but rather to be honest so that you can enter into your journey with eyes wide open and get the support that you need. Also, if you are hoping to support adoptive and foster families, you should understand the unique aspects of their experience.

DAVID AND ALICIA

David and Alicia were stressed out. You could see it in their eyes. There was a weariness about them that didn't seem to go away. It was as if the light and energy in their bodies had been slowly sapped away over time, and now they were just going through the motions, trying to make it through.

It hadn't always been like that. They had a strong foundation in their marriage and loved each other deeply. They met at a university, when David was working on his master's in theology and Alicia was finishing up her bachelor's in early childhood education. Alicia was drawn to David's big smile and charming wit, and David was attracted to Alicia's bubbly personality and ability to connect with anyone. David worked as an associate teaching pastor in a large nondenominational church, and Alicia taught second grade before transitioning to be a stay-at-home mom once they adopted.

During one of her summers in college, Alicia went on a mission trip to Uganda and worked in an orphanage there, which is when she first felt as if God was possibly calling her to care for vulnerable children in a serious way. A few years after they had married, David and Alicia were struggling to get pregnant. Alicia remembered back to her time in Uganda and wondered if perhaps she and David were being called to have a family in a different way. Independently from Alicia, David was introduced to some missionaries who were involved in caring for vulnerable children in China, and their church began a partnership supporting the missionary family. When David and Alicia first talked about it, they were surprised about how God seemed to be working in both of their hearts in the direction of adoption. They began to prayerfully consider whether this might be a step that God wanted them to take, and three years later, they adopted sisters from China. Betsy was four years old, and Lucy was two.

Fast-forward six years, and David and Alicia were struggling. There were definitely moments of joy with their girls. Betsy loved painting, and the refrigerator was often covered with her latest art projects. Lucy enjoyed playing with her dolls and listening to music. David and Alicia relished many of the beautiful aspects of parenting, like cuddling while reading bedtime stories or going to another kid's birthday party. However, David and Alicia also felt maxed out more days than not. Both of their daughters had some significant challenges. Betsy, who was now ten, had issues with hoarding food. She had a hard time focusing on her schoolwork, and it looked like she might need to repeat a grade. She spent many long evenings crying at the dinner table, trying unsuccessfully to understand and complete her homework. Even though Alicia was a teacher by trade and thought she should be able to deal with this sort of issue, it just wasn't working. Betsy had been receiving therapeutic services, including counseling and occupational therapy, but progress was slow. They were working with the school to get Betsy on an Individualized Education Program (IEP), but it was a lot to navigate.

Both Betsy and Lucy, who was now eight, were experiencing some issues related to being adopted. David and Alicia had decided to tell their daughters right away about the adoption, but it seemed like lately they had been asking more questions. The family also lived in a mostly white town, and Betsy and Lucy were attending a school that was mostly white. Most of the time, the sisters were the only Asian children in their classrooms. Sometimes the other children would make fun of them because of their ethnicity. For example, one day Betsy came home crying because a boy in her class had made fun of her and called her "squinty eyes," and she didn't understand why her classmates saw her differently. Alicia called the school, furious. The administrators were responsive, concerned, and supportive, which David and Alicia appreciated, but it didn't change that Betsy and Lucy sometimes felt different and isolated. Being white themselves, David and Alicia tried their best to help the girls navigate these issues. Sometimes the parents thought they should help the girls stay more in touch with their Chinese culture, but the couple didn't really know how to do that.

Parenting was taking a toll on David and Alicia's marriage as well. They attempted to prioritize connecting with each other, but they were often just too busy and tired. Date nights became more spread out as the responsibilities with the girls increased. They started to argue and criticize each other more often, nitpicking about minor things. Sometimes arguments didn't really get resolved; instead, David and Alicia just tried to let things go, too exhausted to work through the issues in an in-depth way.

They didn't seem to get a break. David had his full-time responsibilities at the church, and he started to look forward to going to the office, just to get a break from the chaos at home. Alicia, on the other hand, was responsible for the girls full-time. Sometimes she would get so anxious that she couldn't fall asleep, and she would also wake up worrying about the girls, particularly Betsy and her school problems. Alicia kept thinking that this was only going to be a phase, and things would get better. But a few years had passed, and the stress was starting to get to her. Alicia and David were both losing hope of the situation improving.

STRESS AND HOW IT IMPACTS US

Like David and Alicia, we are often caring so intensely for our children that we forget to care for ourselves. Maybe we want to care for ourselves, but parenthood's demands, particularly with adoptive and foster families, are so high that the task feels completely impossible. But what exactly is happening to our body when we experience chronic stress? Stress is a physiological response that happens in our body in response to a threat or challenge (Lazarus & Folkman, 1984). When we experience stress, our bodies produce higher quantities of certain chemicals, such as cortisol, adrenaline, and noradrenaline. In response to these chemicals, heart rate and blood pressure increase, more blood flows to the muscles, we sweat more, and we have a higher state of alertness. Anything nonessential slows down, such as the digestive and immune systems. All the body's resources are allocated to the systems most needed to deal with the threat or challenge. You may have learned about the "fight, flight, or freeze" response and heard this phrase in your child's counseling room, but the same thing happens for you. The human body is constantly appraising stressful or threatening situations so that we can take appropriate action.

Struggling to deal with the stress in our lives can negatively impact our physical and emotional health. Physical problems linked to stress include back and chest pain, obesity, erectile dysfunction, headache, heart disease, high blood pressure, lowered immunity to fight diseases, muscle aches, nail biting, stomach problems, and sleep difficulties. Emotional problems linked to stress include anger, anxiety, burnout, depression, irritability, difficulty concentrating, restlessness, sadness, and fatigue. Stress has also been associated with eating problems; drug, alcohol, and tobacco use; and relationship difficulties—all told, just about every physical or emotional problem that people experience as human beings. Stress can also exacerbate existing problems. Chronic stress can affect our emotional baseline, inhibiting our ability to make rational decisions or connect with others, including our spouse and children, in healthy ways. We may start to feel like we have a short fuse. We may even look in the mirror one day and not recognize the person we've become.

STRESS ASSOCIATED WITH ADOPTIVE AND FOSTER PARENTING

For foster and adoptive parents, the transition to parenthood is often experienced as challenging and stressful. This transition has the potential to lead to negative psychological and physical health outcomes for the parents, as well as a deleterious effect on the marriage relationship. Whether parents can successfully navigate this transition involves an interactional process between the demands of parenting on one hand and the resources and support on the other (McKay, Ross, & Goldberg, 2010). When the demands of parenting and resources are balanced, the transition to parenthood will be experienced more positively. When the demands of parenting outweigh the resources, however, the adjustment becomes more difficult. When the scales are tipped in this direction for too long, we start to see negative effects of stress psychologically, physically, and relationally.

In what follows, I discuss some of the unique stressors that adoptive and foster parents experience (Groze, 1996). So often adoptive and foster parents feel misunderstood when support systems fail to recognize and empathize with parents' unique challenges. Adoptive and foster parenting are not your average parenting gigs, which most of the world doesn't understand. The healing journey for the precious children who come from hard places can be a lifelong process. As Christians, we need to be willing and able to sit in those hard places with these kids and the parents who are caring for them. Several stressors are common to adoptive and foster parenting, including:

- Trauma
- Attachment
- Cultural context
- Community
- Service system
- Family system
- Parents
- Spirituality

We consider each individually.

Trauma

The behaviors associated with trauma responses can be baffling. I remember sitting with parents who would talk about how their son or daughter would regularly have prolonged temper tantrums lasting over an hour. Children would bang their head against the wall or pull their hair out when they became upset, or would quickly become aggressive with other peers even though they were old enough to know this behavior was not okay. Traumatized children might hoard food in their room even though they are being fed more than enough, or lie, cheat, and steal and—when caught red-handed—never own up to it or show remorse. Some would show no emotions at all even though they had experienced something terrible.

These kinds of behaviors can be very stressful for parents, particularly because of a general misunderstanding of what trauma really is and how it manifests itself in the lives of children who have been through it. We are all aware of more common traumas (e.g., a car accident, moving to a new house in a new city, or death of a loved one), but what about chronic trauma and the effects it has on children over long periods of time? Examples would be starvation or malnutrition, repeated witness to domestic violence, physical or sexual abuse, neglect, and the list goes on and on. These chronic traumas are often overlooked or misunderstood in the context of adoption or foster care because we don't see them clearly. But understanding how chronic trauma manifests itself through a child's behavior or spirit can open up a whole new world of understanding.

Perhaps you are a grandparent, aunt or uncle, friend, or church leader who has a relationship with an adoptive or foster family. You observe the parenting style taking place, and it may seem too lenient or forgiving. Maybe you've had thoughts that if only the children had more consequences, they wouldn't act this way. Or you may have thought, *I have no idea what to do right now,* and pull away. These reactions are common when we don't understand trauma.

What is trauma? *Trauma* is an emotional response to a terrible event. Perhaps you are caring for a child who was exposed to alcohol or drugs in utero, physically abused, sexually abused, exposed to domestic violence, neglected, experienced a medical trauma (e.g., spent time in the NICU after birth), experienced the loss of a loved one, or experienced a stressful pregnancy in utero. All these traumatic experiences can affect a child's brain development (Purvis et al., 2013). A child who has experienced abuse receives the message, "I do not like you." A child experiencing neglect gets the message, "You do not exist."

Trauma changes the brain. Simply understanding this truth can bring about a whole new sense of understanding and validation for parents. For example, in her book *Emerging with Wings: A True Story of Lies, Pain, and the Love That Heals*, Danielle Bernock (2014) writes, "Trauma is personal. It does not disappear if it is not validated. When it is ignored or invalidated the silent screams continue internally heard only by the one held captive. When someone enters the pain and hears the screams healing can begin" (p. 146).

Trauma and the brain. Some parents ask, "But I received my child at birth. How could she have experienced any trauma?" Great question. As babies develop in their mother's womb, they are able to learn, feel, taste, touch, and hear. Various research studies have demonstrated that infants are able to recognize and show a preference for songs or books they heard while in utero (Hopson, 1998). We also know that a pregnant mother's emotional state affects her baby. The neurotransmitters being released in the mother's body reach the child's brain. If a mother experiences high levels of stress and anxiety, she releases hormones such as cortisol in what's called a *metabolic cascade*, which affects her immune system and the baby in utero. Chronic anxiety for the mother exposes the child to these stress hormones, which is traumatic for a baby in utero. Conversely, when a mother is happy and healthy, she releases oxytocin, which communicates to the unborn child, "I'm safe, and it is peaceful here."

A mother who is considering adoption for her baby or who was exposed to domestic violence during the pregnancy is probably very stressed, and her baby is experiencing that stress as well. Moreover, memories are encoded in brain cells, impacting the child's neuro-development. Our bodies keep score. Even though the child has no memory of this experience, the brain's neurobiology has stored it.

When a child experiences trauma, the amygdala takes over. The amygdala is the emotional part of the brain, and it deals with survival and protection. When the amygdala gets activated, all other areas of the brain are turned off. Often a child impacted by adoption or foster care isn't willfully trying to be defiant; it's a hardware issue in the brain. It's like you're trying to get your child to press the brake while the child has the gas pedal pressed to the floor. Dan Siegel and Tina Payne Bryson (2012) have compared the brain to a house. We have our upstairs brain and our downstairs brain. The upstairs brain represents thinking, and the downstairs brain represents emotion. In children with a history of trauma, the amygdala—the emotional center—is often firing on all cylinders. The downstairs brain has taken over the house. Meanwhile, the upstairs part of the brain responsible for things like emotional regulation, language, and executive functioning gets turned off.

How trauma impacts behavior. Children impacted by adoption or foster care have often experienced trauma that drives their emotions and behavior, whether they remember it or not. A child who has been in your care for quite some time may still have past trauma that impacts current thoughts, feelings, and behaviors. There is a difference between a child *knowing* he is safe and *feeling* he is safe.

Consider this example: Imagine you are a soldier in combat. You hear gunfire and immediately drop to the ground to keep safe. Your heart is beating incredibly fast. You are doing what it takes to survive. This goes on for months. Every time you're in this situation, every time you hear gunfire, you drop to the ground. The shots are close. Your senses are heightened. You're on high alert. And then it happens. You get shot in the arm. You're terrified and in pain. A medic comes to bandage you up and takes you to safety.

After some time, you're sent back home for further medical care and rehabilitation. You've been back home for a few months, and the transition has been pretty hard. You're struggling with nightmares and feel hyperalert wherever you go. One particular day you are on your way home and stop at local grocery store to buy some milk. You've got your carton of milk and are heading back to your car, enjoying the sunshine on your face, when you hear a car backfire. *Bang!* Instinctively you drop to the ground. Although you know in your head you are safe in the suburbs, your past trauma is still driving your behavior. This is what I mean by *knowing* you're safe and *feeling* safe. Your children often have trauma-affected brains that continue to drive their behavior, and feeling safe may take a very long time.

Kids who have experienced trauma are not bad children. What is sometimes viewed as intentional or defiant behavior is more of a "can't" than a "won't." They have been deeply wounded. Their symptoms are the truth they are not yet able to speak. Difficult behaviors or reactions, such as hoarding food, aggressive behavior, and running away, are often the result of past trauma. Because of this, we all need to view our child's behavior through a trauma lens. Parents as well as the broader support community need to become more trauma-informed.

Trauma can impact children differently depending on age. Infants who experience trauma do not have the words to describe the event or their feelings, but they can retain memories of sights, sounds, and smells. They may react by being irritable, crying more than usual, or wanting to be held or cuddled. Preschool-age children may react to trauma by feeling helplessness, powerlessness, or intense fear and insecurity about being separated from caregivers. They may act out or have prolonged episodes of dysregulation and difficulty calming down. They might also experience physical symptoms (e.g., stomachaches) or engage in repetitive play themes. I remember working with a four-year-old girl who had been physically abused, and her play theme in therapy was a little baby who was always sick and couldn't get better.

Elementary- and middle-school children can experience a wide range of emotions and reactions—sadness, fear, guilt, and anger. Teenagers also experience a range of emotions and reactions but may be more likely than younger children to withdraw, want to be alone, and lose interest in school, friends, and hobbies. Children who have experienced trauma may also regress to an earlier age. While these reactions are common, each child's response to traumatic life events is unique.

Adoptive or foster parents who begin to understand the effects of trauma can sometimes start to feel hopeless. One parent said to me, "If the trauma my daughter experienced is still running her life today, is there any hope for her to live a normal life? It seems like the trauma is in the driver's seat and just won't let up." Part of the reason I wrote this book is to help parents in situations like these. Effective strategies are available to help children work through their trauma experiences.

A traumatized brain, or *trauma brain*, can experience healing because of plasticity. *Brain plasticity* refers to the ability of the brain to change, adapt, and create new neural connections over time with different experiences. Just because a child is struggling right now doesn't mean the child will struggle in the same way forever. Kids impacted by adoption and foster care can grow and blossom into the beautiful people God designed them to be. I firmly believe that what is happening with your kids right now is not necessarily an indication of their future.

If your child has fetal alcohol spectrum disorder (FASD), for example, that may be his diagnosis, but it is not his identity. If your daughter has attachment issues as a result of significant abuse early in her life, or from bouncing around in foster homes, that trauma she has gone through does not define who she is or how her future will look. Your children are precious. Remember, it's not you versus your child's behavior, but you and your children together facing their trauma (Purvis et al., 2007).

Attachment

Attachment—the emotional bond between parent and infant (Ainsworth, 1973; Bowlby, 1969) during the first few months of life—is important because it serves as a blueprint for relationships with others. This attachment dance between a baby and caregiver is important. When a baby has a need, the baby voices that need by crying. When the caregiver responds to those cries and comforts the baby, the baby develops trust. The baby begins to learn from a caregiver how to self-regulate. Babies also learn that their caregivers are a secure base. An infant who experiences consistent, nurturing love and affection from caregivers learns that her needs will be met. Trust is formed, and a secure attachment is likely to develop. Children learn at a neurobiological level that when they cry, their caregiver comes and takes care of their needs. The baby processes the message: *I feel protected, I feel heard, I have worth, and my physical and emotional needs are taken care of.*

On the other hand, when a caregiver is distant, misattuned, emotionally unavailable, unresponsive, or intrusive, these behaviors can cause children to experience considerable distress. As a result, they adapt to the messaging they receive from distant caregivers by building defensive attachment strategies in an effort to feel safe, modulate intense emotions, and reduce frustration and pain. This process interrupts their ability to learn the necessary regulatory skills. Some of our children had a need and cried, but no one came. Perhaps they were raised in an orphanage that could not possibly provide all the care and nurture to every child. Survival instincts kick in: *I can trust no one but myself, I'm responsible for my own survival.* These experiences can lead an infant to develop insecure attachment issues.

When children have difficulty forming a secure attachment, two key problems arise that can lead to increased stress levels for the children and family. First, these children rarely feel safe. Because they did not experience their initial primary caregiver as a secure base, they view caregivers and the world as dangerous. Children with insecure attachment tend to be more on guard and defensive than securely attached children. The former may have a hard time relaxing, sleeping, and playing with others.

Second, a big part of a baby developing a secure attachment involves being consistently comforted when in distress. Babies who develop insecure attachment tend not to trust that their needs will be met when they cry out. Instead, they feel on their own in life. Growing up, they likely will have a more difficult time trusting others, including adoptive or foster parents, to meet their needs. They also may have more difficulty being comforted and settling down when they are upset.

In the general population, about 40 percent of children have insecure attachment (Moullin, Waldfogel, & Washbrook, 2014). However, placing children outside their own home is itself often associated with disruptions in attachment relationships (Troutman, Ryan, & Cardi, 2000). Children in foster care are more likely to present with insecure attachment than are children who are not adopted or fostered, although they show higher levels of secure attachment than children raised in institutions (Quiroga & Hamilton-Giachritsis, 2016).

Reading these statistics can cause anyone to feel overwhelmed or even hopeless. But there is hope. Throughout the chapters ahead, we share honest stories of families who have faced big obstacles, but also the hope they have found through community connection, understanding trauma, and shifting their perspective from the hard parts of this journey to the kingdom impact they are making in the lives of the children they are parenting.

What you are doing through foster care or adoption is good. Remember and believe that you are changing the lives of vulnerable children. The goal for this book is for you to not only see this in your own journey but embrace it and apply this belief to everything you do as a parent.

Cultural and Social Context

For many people and in many communities, a social stigma still comes with adoption and foster care. For example, some children feel a deep sense of shame, abandonment, or unwantedness when their birth parents are unwilling or unable to care for them. This stigma can be communicated to adoptive and foster parents and children from other family members, friends, schools, and the culture at large. Adoptive and foster families may also struggle with this stigma internally, even if they maintain a positive attitude on the outside. An eight-year-old boy in foster care told me he felt like he couldn't tell anyone he was a foster child. He felt embarrassed and ashamed, keeping it a secret from all his school friends. He didn't want his foster parents to pick him up from school because he was afraid his peers would begin asking questions.

Adoptive and foster families may also be transracial, meaning parenting a child from a different racial or ethnic background. Difficulties can come with this situation also, including decisions about helping the child integrate or staying in touch with the cultural background of the family of origin. This was certainly a challenge for David and Alicia. They were caught off guard by the challenges associated with raising children from a different ethnicity. Being white, they weren't in touch with racism's prevalence in their community. They listened and tried to be supportive when Betsy and Lucy described being made fun of in school for looking different, but because they didn't share that experience, David and Alicia weren't sure how to help their daughters handle it. While community support is important, community can also serve as a stressor if the family lives in a less tolerant, less forgiving, or less informed area.

Community

Many adoptive and foster parents struggle with role ambiguity and lack good role models for what it means to be an adoptive or foster parent. For parents who are giving birth to children, community rituals serve to strengthen the community and bind the parents and children together. Adoptive and foster parents often lack these rituals. For example, baby showers may not happen for adoptive and foster parents. Church baby dedications might gloss over a family who has recently adopted a child. In Indiana, where coauthor Mike is from, a couple both worked for a large church, and when they adopted their little girl from India, the church leadership denied maternity leave for the mother, causing her to have to take vacation days. The community, friends, and family in general might also demonstrate a lack of support. For example, explicit or implicit suggestions that parents "give the children back" when the going gets tough or statements such as "You did this to yourself" can be disheartening to parents. Finally, the broader culture's use of language, such as calling birth parents the "natural parents" or "real parents," can further accentuate the divide between adoptive and biological families.

In addition, one's extended family and friends can have a negative influence on adoptive and foster families. Sometimes traditional parenting values are imposed on adoptive and foster parents, and negative feedback or advice is often given. Over time, this causes the buildup of enormous amounts of stress.

David and Alicia navigated some of these difficulties when they adopted Betsy and Lucy. For example, Alicia was in the process of planning a baby shower for her cousin when she realized that no one had thought to plan a baby shower for her when they were adopting the girls. Now she felt sad and hurt. Was it the fact that she adopted? Or because the girls were older when they came home? Was the addition to their family not as special or worthy to be celebrated? Or did their family not know how to celebrate adoption? Also, their extended family was mostly supportive, but there was a definite lack of empathy sometimes when Betsy and Lucy were really struggling. For example, Alicia's mother gave a lot of advice that David and Alicia had already tried, so it felt invalidating to hear the same suggestions repeated.

Service System

Adoptive and foster parents often have to deal with a long period of preparation and waiting before they actually bring a child into their home. The home-study process can be stressful. A lot of uncertainty is involved with the waiting process, and sometimes parents are given hope that they will receive a child, only to have it fall through and they must enter yet another stretch into the unknown. Some states have a forty-eight-hour waiting period during which a birth mother can change her mind about the adoption. I've watched adoptive parents hold their new baby in their arms—experiencing the joy of parenthood, smelling their new child, giving him a name—only to have the agency worker take the infant and return him to his birth mother.

Also, many service agencies do not provide enough training and support for adoptive and foster parents, so they may feel unprepared.

Service agency training often centers around particular state laws and regulations but fails to talk practically about trauma, common problems that arise, or the power of connecting to other understanding parents. Moreover, adoptive and foster parents often deal with having incomplete or no information about their child, which can create difficulties for parents in understanding and meeting their child's specific needs. Many adoptive parents commiserate over the lack of medical, mental health, and social information available about their child. Even simple tasks like filling out the history form at the doctor's office or completing an elementary school family-tree project can be a source of pain.

Many adoptive and foster parents also deal with service providers who aren't fully trained in adoption-related, foster-related, and trauma-related issues. For example, they may engage with therapists or others who lack knowledge about the most effective ways to work with children who have survived trauma. Advocating for your child's needs can become daunting and overwhelming.

Additionally, child welfare workers (e.g., caseworkers) are often significantly overworked and underpaid, leading to high amounts of burnout and turnover. Families often find themselves working with several different caseworkers over the course of a year or two. This turnover takes a toll on caseworkers, families, and ultimately the children they work alongside as it reaffirms abandonment experiences children have that adults are unreliable, reaffirms the children's emotional experiences that they are not lovable and do not have worth, and can be frustrating as caseworkers need to quickly get familiar with a case history to effectively do their job and sometimes make crucial decisions about case outcomes.

Finally, the fees associated with adoptive and foster care can cause added stress. The adoption process can be very expensive for families. Adoptive parents sometimes take out loans or expend a lot of time and energy on fundraising efforts to cover the steep fees. And the financial stress often doesn't stop there. Families are surprised by the ongoing expenses that they can incur postplacement: medical appointments, ongoing therapy bills, and in some cases out-of-home treatment. I've worked with families who have taken out second mortgages or had to delay their retirement to cover these expenses. This financial strain can cause tension between spouses and between parents and kids.

Regarding foster care, the subsidies for foster families can add complexity to an already fraught situation. First, the subsidies and support can be insufficient to meet the foster child's needs. Some foster parents struggle to advocate for their child to receive resources to cover necessary services, such as occupational or physical therapy. Second, in some situations, the subsidies can encourage parents to enter foster care with the intention to "foster-to-adopt," in order to avoid the expenses associated with adoption, which can lead to problems with foster families working against attempts to reunify children with their birth families.

David and Alicia were often frustrated with the service system. Before they brought Betsy and Lucy home, they were close to adopting a young boy from China, only to have the adoption fall through. David and Alicia, who were so excited about beginning their new family only to have it delayed again, were devastated. It became hard to hold the longing and anticipation in their hearts. Also, the fees associated with adoption were almost prohibitive for David and Alicia. David worked as a pastor, and Alicia as a teacher, so they were not wealthy by any means. The cost associated with adoption stretched their finances, which caused additional stress for their family.

Family System

Some challenges associated with adoption and foster parenting relate to how the existing family operates and relates to one another. Imagine your own family of origin. Think about how you interacted with your parents and siblings. What were the unspoken rules? What role did each family member play? How did your parents encourage or correct you? We all have family experiences that shape and inform our parenting strategies, whether we are fully aware of them or not. Perhaps you grew up in a home that was not affectionate, and hugs, kisses, and talking about feelings were not part of the interaction. Maybe you grew up in a family with many fun traditions. Perhaps when you misbehaved, you were grounded or received consequences. When you consider your own childhood, are there parallels to how you now parent your children? Most often, our default parenting strategy is based on the ways we were raised.

When a family brings a child impacted by the loss of the child's first family home for the first time, the child steps into a set of established rules and relationship dynamics. (The child may also be used to a set of rules and dynamics from their previous caregivers, which may or may not match the current family norms.) Some of these rules and dynamics can be helpful, and others can make things more difficult.

We may have unconscious expectations about what the adoption or foster care journey will look like, or how our child will behave or how the family will interact. Then reality sets in. Even seemingly reasonable expectations such as "my child will obey" or "my child will tell me she loves me" are sometimes unrealistic, at least at first, for children affected by trauma. Some families may have expectations that their child will be grateful toward them for rescuing or saving them from their previous situation. When high expectations conflict with the realities of adoptive and foster parenting, especially for children who may struggle with emotional or behavioral problems or have special needs, stress can increase.

Also, family systems that are rigid—with specific rules for how a parent or child should act or behave—may have difficulty adapting to the changing needs of their child impacted by adoption or foster care. Research shows that consequence- and punitive-oriented approaches may keep children functioning in their trauma brain and not bring them the healing they need (Purvis et al., 2007).

Adding a child also results in adjustments for the other children already in the home. Sometimes parents have a hard time connecting with their children in the same way as before. Also, children through birth, adoption, or foster care may have different needs, and parents can struggle with how best to meet the unique needs of each child.

Finally, lack of adequate support systems can exacerbate family stress. Families are often left more or less alone, without enough emotional, informational, or tangible support. Sometimes parents recognize and alter their expectations, and when the support networks do not, this can leave families feeling alone, isolated, and misunderstood. This key observation led to the idea behind this book, and I focus on developing these support systems throughout the rest of the chapters.

Expectations was one area where David and Alicia had to make a big shift. Being a teacher by profession, Alicia had high expectations that her girls would succeed in school, and also that she would be able to help her girls with whatever education-related issues came up for them. As they went along, however, Betsy and Lucy clearly were experiencing difficulties outside of Alicia's control, abilities, or expertise. Alicia needed to become more flexible with her expectations of Betsy and Lucy, meeting them where they were and being the support they needed. For Alicia, she had to let go of viewing Betsy's and Lucy's school performance as a reflection of her parenting. Instead, Alicia worked on acknowledging that we all have a unique set of strengths and weaknesses—and that's okay. As Alicia worked through some of her own issues related to expectations, she was better able to love Betsy and Lucy as they were, which improved their relationships and their stress levels.

Parents

Some stressors have to do with a parent's individual experiences. Some parents enter the adoption or foster journey following experiences with infertility. Although the adoption or foster process is often a joyful time, feelings of sadness or anger can also arise about the failure to have biological children. Some parents also have histories of abuse or trauma, which can be triggered when parenting children with similar histories or experiences. Also, some adoptive or foster parents enter this journey at an older age than parents who have biological children. As a result, they may have more challenges maintaining the energy necessary to keep up with young children, and they also may feel out of step with their friends and community, who may have had children at a younger age. Additionally, the parents of their children's friends may be younger as well, and connecting with these parents socially can be more difficult.

Infertility was the primary reason that David and Alicia entered into their adoption journey in the first place. They expected that when they adopted their daughters, the pain and sadness associated with infertility would disappear because they longed to be parents. Much to their surprise, they would occasionally find the pain and sadness reappearing, even when things were going well with their daughters. They loved their daughters deeply, but had unresolved grief. They came to understand that the journey of processing infertility was more long-term, not something that would be "solved" with adoption. One thing that helped David and Alicia was attending counseling to work through some of their own issues regarding infertility. As David and Alicia were able to process some of their sadness and loss about not being able to have biological children, they found themselves more grateful for the family they did have and better able to appreciate their own unique journey and experience.

Spirituality

Finally, some parents experience stressors associated with religion and spirituality. Christians and churches strongly encourage and celebrate caring for vulnerable children, which often happens through adoption and foster care. I discuss some good reasons for this support in greater detail in the next chapter. However, this religious or spiritual motivation can also lead to some issues and problems. Adoptive and foster parents may start out without enough information or knowledge about what they're doing. They may believe that, if they follow God's plan for adopting or fostering, it will all work out or have a positive outcome. When the reality of their situation is markedly different from their expectations, parents may blame or become angry with God, or experience spiritual struggles (Exline et al., 2014). David and Alicia experienced spiritual highs and lows on their adoption journey. They definitely felt deep in their soul that adoption was something God wanted them to do, so they had a sense that adoption was part of their mission and that God was with them through the ups and the downs. However, they also sometimes struggled spiritually when things were really tough. Tough questions came to mind: Had God abandoned them? Why wasn't God coming through in this area?

COPING WITH STRESS

As we have seen, adoption and foster care can lead to stress in many forms. It's easy for the stressors and demands to overwhelm existing supports and resources. If this situation continues too long, conditions can quickly spiral downward, leading to negative outcomes such as failed placements and marital dissolution. How can adoptive and foster parents put themselves and their children in the best position to live a full, healthy, vibrant life?

A big part of the solution is to work on increasing resources and supports for parents—the focus of the remainder of this book. But adoptive and foster parents can work the other side of the equation as well—reducing the level of stress, as well as the negative effects that stress has on our mental and physical health. My model for reducing and limiting stress has four steps: informed expectations, boundaries and limits, adaptive appraisal, and considerate coping.

Informed Expectations

First, prospective parents need to enter into the adoption or foster care process with informed expectations. You don't want to be caught off guard. Too many adoptive and foster parents begin with beautiful intentions and then are blindsided when realities clash with expectations. When people wanted to follow Jesus, he told them to "count the costs" (Luke 14:28). In the same way, adoption and foster care are beautiful, but there are costs. Learn and prepare, as much as possible, for what is likely to come your way.

One of the reasons David and Alicia experienced so much stress, at least at the beginning of their journey, is because they were unprepared for what was about to happen. They didn't have a clear understanding of the stressors associated with adopting internationally. In a way, the stressors blindsided them at first. Once they became more informed about some of the realities and challenges, they realized that some of Betsy's and Lucy's problems, such as difficulties in school, were within normal limits for children who were adopted internationally. Having more informed expectations allowed them to moderate some of their stress. It didn't disappear, but they didn't feel so alone or blame themselves for being bad parents.

When coauthor Mike Berry and his wife, Kristin, first started out on this journey, they had a mountain of questions but no answers.

This led them to formulate glamorized expectations, which were later dashed when they came face-to-face with the trauma their children were going through. It took years before they finally learned better techniques and practices. Had they begun the process more informed, their first several years as foster and adoptive parents would have been much more successful.

Boundaries and Limits

Setting and maintaining appropriate boundaries and limits in your adoptive and foster journey are crucial steps. Boundaries involve identifying and differentiating between what is within and what is outside our responsibility (Cloud & Townsend, 1992). Boundaries help us take control of our own lives and free us to let other people take responsibility for their own lives. Sometimes we can get into trouble by taking on more responsibility for other people's decisions, or someone may ask us to make a commitment we know we don't have the time or energy for, but we say yes anyway, desiring to avoid disapproval from another. For example, we might say yes to a placement because of a sense of urgency and desire for every child to experience the love and safety of a family. Or we feel an obligation, thinking, *If not me, then who?* When we don't have clear boundaries and we can't place appropriate limits on ourselves or other people, we take on additional and unnecessary stress.

For example, part of the reason that David and Alicia decided to adopt two girls and not more children was that two children felt like it was about the most they could handle at this time in their life. If their resources had been different, they may have made a different decision. But they were okay with honestly evaluating their limits and drawing a boundary about what they felt they could reasonably take on as a family.

Going back to the Berry family for a moment, in 2012, when they adopted their youngest son, they decided also to end their foster care license. For parents who have big hearts for caring for vulnerable children, this can seem contradictory to the reason they signed up for foster care and adoption in the first place. Everyone has limitations, though, and sometimes pushing forward and ignoring healthy boundaries can do more damage than good. The Berrys realized they were at their limit when they finalized their son's adoption. To keep taking additional placements would have been detrimental to them and, more importantly, to their children. If you have wrestled over this or struggled to set healthy boundaries for yourself, let the Berrys' story encourage you and release you from guilt.

Adaptive Appraisal

Our perception or appraisal of the stressful situation is important (Lazarus & Folkman, 1984). For example, one big distinction is whether we view a stressful situation as a challenge or a threat. In general, viewing stressful events as challenges leads to more positive outcomes, whereas viewing stressful events as threats leads to more negative outcomes. Viewing stressful situations as negative or bad is pretty normal, but your obstacle can also offer opportunities for growth (Holiday, 2014). We've all been in that situation where we're dealing with something really difficult, and the annoying person at church says, "Well, you know that 'in all things God works for the good of those who love him and who have been called according to his purpose' [Romans 8:28]. You just gotta keep the faith!" This kind of platitude isn't generally perceived as helpful.

That said, in my own life, I have found two benefits that sometimes occur when I encounter a stressful situation, provided I'm willing to engage the experience and not avoid it. First, engaging with stress can help build certain character strengths or virtues, similar to the idea of going to the gym. In order to get stronger, you have to put your muscles under strain. In a similar way, if you want to grow in virtues such as patience, love, and humility, the best way is to engage with experiences that force you to work on that virtue. Second, engaging with stress can better enable you to connect and empathize with others who are struggling. In order to give grace, you have to be able to receive grace for yourself. In order to receive grace for yourself, you need to have experienced some measure of pain, brokenness, and struggle. This is one of the greatest benefits of engaging with stressful situations in your life. You open yourself up to be in vulnerable community with others who are also struggling.

Considerate Coping

You should develop a set of effective coping strategies for the stress that presents for yourself and your family. Coping involves cognitive, emotional, and behavioral efforts to manage the stressful events or circumstances. How do you manage the stress in your life? So many times, we work with our kids to help them develop effective coping strategies, but we forget that the same principles apply to us. I have a few suggestions for figuring out how to effectively apply your coping strategies when you need them the most. To begin with, a wide variety of coping strategies is best, because sometimes a strategy that works in one situation doesn't work elsewhere. (See table 1 for a list of potential coping strategies.)

The two main types of coping strategies are problem-focused and emotion-focused (Billings & Moos, 1981). Problem-focused strategies try to do something to modify or eliminate the stress through one's behavior, such as getting more information, planning, and taking action. For example, you might have your child in counseling to work through your child's trauma experiences, attend training for how to effectively parent children who exhibit aggressive behaviors as a result of trauma experiences, or advocate for an IEP at school to support your child's learning needs. In general, problem-focused strategies are an effective way to deal with stressors, and I would

TABLE 1. COPING STRATEGIES	
Problem-Focused	**Emotion-Focused**
Attending training on trauma or attachment-based parenting	Praying
Attending a conference on adoption and foster parenting	Journaling
Participating in family counseling	Participating in family counseling
Meeting with your child's teacher to discuss concerns at school	Exercising
Meeting with your child's school for an Individualized Education Program (IEP)	Reading a good book
Putting together a plan with your child for an important upcoming transition	Meditating
Role-playing a challenging situation	Talking with a friend or family member
Brainstorming solutions to a problem	Spending time in nature

recommend starting there. For example, David and Alicia found that they could do some things (e.g., adapt parenting strategies for trauma-related behavior, get more intensive help or therapy for their children) that could help them to address the problems at hand, and thus reduce the amount of stress they experienced. If something can actually help solve the problem, get that process started.

But sometimes solving the problem isn't possible. Things happen in the adoption and foster care process that are outside of your control. For example, you might be like David and Alicia, who were parenting a child with some significant developmental delays. There may be a limit in your problem-solving capabilities. This is where emotion-focused coping strategies really shine. If implemented well, they allow you to achieve a level of peace and well-being even if the stressful situation can't be solved. This type of coping and self-care is *crucial*.

Emotion-focused coping tries to reduce the negative emotional response that stress causes us. We can do this in healthy ways, such as talking about emotions, praying, meditating, or journaling, and in unhealthy ways, such as avoiding the situation, eating, or using drugs or alcohol. In general, emotion-focused coping strategies that involve distancing or avoidance—which can be as simple as distracting yourself by watching TV—are less helpful in the long term, although they can sometimes provide short-term relief. On the other hand, emotion-focused strategies that involve engaging one's emotions, seeking out support, and connecting with others are more likely to be effective.

We often have a hard time prioritizing self-care over the care we need to give our child. However, self-care helps you cope with your stress, which ultimately gives you a better emotional baseline for parenting. Think about self-care like breathing. If you are only breathing *out* (giving care to others), you will not survive. Likewise, if you are only breathing *in* (giving care to yourself), you will not survive either. Caring for yourself and for others needs to be balanced for you to thrive. Also, even if you are facing a stressful situation in which problem-focused coping may be helpful, the problem-solving process may take a significant amount of time.

With a lot of our children, there's no quick or easy fix to what they've experienced. Emotion-focused coping strategies can help you survive and thrive as you work through the process of solving your problems. To help them deal with the mounting stress in their lives, David and Alicia identified different kinds of emotion-focused coping strategies that worked best for them. David enjoyed physical exercise; nothing made him feel better than getting out on the trails and going for a hard run. Alicia, on the other hand, experienced a lot of relief through journaling and prayer. By committing to their coping strategies on a regular basis, David and Alicia were able to maintain their sanity even when their circumstances were difficult.

One final thing about using religion and spirituality as a coping tool: faith can be incredibly helpful and comforting when dealing with stress. Prayer can help us receive comfort and support from God. Worship can connect us to God in a deep and intimate way. Reading scripture can bring clarity and comfort as we connect with the teachings and experiences of Jesus and other people of faith. Being in a close-knit faith community where you can receive love and support can be incredibly helpful. But some ways of using religion are less helpful, and some ways of engaging with God can actually leave you in a worse spot than you were before.

For example, connecting a difficult circumstance with your past sinful actions can heap guilt and shame on top of an already difficult situation (e.g., "My family is struggling right now because I had an abortion several years ago"). Relying on God for a miracle to fix a situation, such as healing a child, can sometimes result in disillusionment and spiritual disruption if the desired outcome does not come to pass. The key is to engage with God in a balanced way that works with your other coping strategies rather than against them. It can also be helpful to check out your coping strategies with wise counsel from professional helpers and other Christians.

Exercise: Stress, Appraisal, and Coping

Take out a sheet of paper and find a place where you can be quiet and have some time by yourself. Think about a stressful situation that is going on in your life. Write a few sentences describing the stressful event:

_____

_____

_____

_____

_____

_____

_____

Next, think about the boundaries and limits you have set up in your life. Are there any boundaries or limits you could implement to reduce your level of stress? Write a few sentences about how you might work toward developing healthier boundaries and limits in your life:

_____

_____

_____

_____

_____

_____

_____

_____

Spend a few minutes thinking about how you are perceiving this stressful event. What is *threatening* about it?

_____

_____

_____

_____

_____

_____

_____

Try to shift gears and think about the stressful event in a different way. What is *challenging* for you about it?

_____

_____

_____

_____

_____

_____

Consider whether this obstacle is presenting any benefits or oppor- tunities. For example, might engaging with this stressful event improve your character? Do you think it could help you connect with others who are struggling? If you stick with it, might this stressful event bring your family together and strengthen your bond with each other?

Now spend some time thinking about the other side of the equa- tion. What resources do you and your family bring to the table that could help you deal with this stressful event? What kinds of help or support could you use in order to deal with the stress?

Think about how you might cope with this stressful event. First, how much control do you have over it?

_____

_____

_____

_____

_____

_____

What are some problem-focused coping strategies you might try in order to deal with this stressor?

_____

_____

_____

_____

_____

_____

What are some emotion-focused coping strategies you might try?

_____

_____

_____

_____

_____

_____

What are some religious coping strategies you might try?

_____

_____

_____

_____

_____

_____

CHAPTER 3

Discerning the Christian Call to Care for Vulnerable Children

*Religion that God our Father accepts as pure and faultless is this:
to look after orphans and widows in their distress.*

—JAMES 1:27A

As a Christian, a big draw for me to commit my life to helping serve children impacted by adoption or foster care and their families is God's call and emphasis to care for vulnerable children, which was one of the reasons I first went into the field of psychology. I felt deeply God's concern for children who were hurting, abandoned, or forgotten. Helping vulnerable children and children in need seemed to be about as close to the heart of God as I could get. Assisting these kids and their families was a mission I could engage with my whole heart. I wanted to partner with God to play a role in this healing process.

Can you relate to this motivation? If you are currently an adoptive or foster parent, what initially drove you to foster or adopt? If you are involved in helping support adoptive and foster families, what drew you to that? Maybe faith is an important aspect of your life and you have felt a call. Even if you aren't religious or you practice a different faith, of course you can still long to help these families.

I spend some time in this chapter discussing the Christian call to serve vulnerable children. I absolutely believe that caring for children from hard places or who have lost their first family is deeply important to the heart of God, and I want to share some of that as an encouragement to you. I also have seen families struggle with their religious or spiritual beliefs on their adoptive or foster parenting journey. Adoptive and foster parenting can affect our faith in a variety of ways. Maybe you feel like your faith is being put to the test or you've lost hope, or perhaps the experience has enabled you to dive deeper into your walk with God.

Let's discuss some of the common religious and spiritual experiences that families face as they parent children from hard places.

GRAYSON AND LESLIE

Grayson and Leslie weren't the type of people who attributed everything that happened in their lives as being God-ordained or providential, but something about adoption was different. From the time she was a little girl, Leslie had always had a heart for kids, especially those in need. In grade school, Leslie was the girl who looked for other kids who were struggling and invited them to sit with her at the lunch table or played with them at recess. Throughout junior high and high school, she spent her summers working as a camp counselor, and in college she volunteered working with inner-city kids. Caring for children in need was always something that was core to who she was and how she felt God had made her.

When she first met Grayson a couple years after graduating college, one of the first things that attracted her to him was how he engaged with kids. He volunteered as a leader in the high school youth group at their church. He also came from a big family and was always hanging out with his siblings and their children. After Leslie and Grayson fell in love and got married, they knew they wanted a big family, but they weren't exactly sure how that was going to look. Because of her connections working with at-risk youth, Leslie was keenly aware of the number of kids who didn't have families themselves and struggled because of their isolation and lack of love and support. The couple questioned whether they should have biological kids when so many kids out there already needed a loving home. The need was so great, and they wondered if God wanted them to play a part in meeting it.

They began a process of trying to discern God's will for their family. Everything was on the table: having biological children, adopting, fostering, or doing a combination. They invited their family, friends, and church community into the journey with them. Specifically, they met with other Christians whom they felt had the gift of wisdom and discernment and told them about their heart for kids, especially those in need. They explained the choices they were considering and asked their community to be in prayer with them. Finally, they spent time praying and reading scripture, individually and as a couple.

They took their time with this process, not wanting to rush into anything. But throughout, Leslie and Grayson felt a strong, consistent message that adoption was something God wanted them to pursue. They had a heart for adoption, individually and together. When they read the scriptures, they saw a strong emphasis throughout the Bible on love, mercy, justice, and meeting the needs of the "least of these," as well as a clear command to care for the vulnerable children among us. Their Christian community was mostly positive in their advice and opinions as well. Not many people in their church community had adopted, but almost every person believed it was a good, noble endeavor, and they encouraged Grayson and Leslie to go for it. In their prayer time, also, Grayson and Leslie felt a strong emotional connection and call to adopt. Of all the things in their life, they had been the most serious about pursuing God's will about whether they should adopt, and they felt like his answer was a clear yes.

Like most adoptive and foster parents, their journey had its ups and downs. They ended up adopting a sibling group of three—Brian (age thirteen), Luke (age seven), and Lisa (age five). Their family changed overnight, and their lives were turned upside down. The time was life-giving but challenging. All three kids had experience in the foster care system and had abandonment issues. Brian had been physically abused in one of his previous placements. Luke had some learning and attention problems that affected his school time. Lisa had developmental delays; she hadn't started school yet, but Leslie had a feeling that a struggle lay ahead.

Grayson and Leslie felt like God was with them, but they had doubts. One issue was how much stress they experienced in the transition to becoming adoptive parents. They figured taking in three kids at once would be tough, but they didn't really know what they were getting themselves into. At times it just felt like too much; these parents were overwhelmed and felt very much alone. They had family members and friends in the area, but no one really understood adoption. Their friends and family thought the issues facing adopted kids were pretty much the same as those facing biological kids, so they didn't quite understand what Grayson and Leslie were experiencing. For example, Brian tended to lash out at Grayson and Leslie when they tried to correct or discipline him. Leslie knew it was his trauma brain talking, but she still sometimes felt scared and out of control. Luke often would retreat into himself and not want to talk about what was bothering him or even make eye contact with Grayson and Leslie. Grayson and especially Leslie longed for some positive affirmation that their parenting was making a difference. A hug or an "I love you" now and then from the kids would have gone a long way.

Grayson and Leslie reached a spiritual low point a few years after the adoption. Brian was a junior in high school and hanging out with a group of friends his parents didn't approve of. There was a lot of conflict and yelling in the home, and Brian would sometimes just blatantly disobey them. At one point, Brian and a few of his friends were arrested for vandalizing the high school at night. Grayson and

Leslie were frustrated and embarrassed. In addition to the parenting and legal difficulties they were going through, they started to feel angry at God. They were so sure that they were doing what God wanted them to do. Had they heard God incorrectly? They had tried their best, but they weren't perfect parents. Sometimes they messed up and were selfish with their kids. Was God punishing them for their sins and struggles? This didn't seem like the God they knew, but Grayson and Leslie were confused about what God was trying to teach them.

Perhaps you have wrestled with these same thoughts or are in a very challenging season right now. You are not alone. In a blog post, Jason Johnson (2016) emphasized a key word in a scripture verse that really struck me: "Well done, good and *faithful* servant" (Matthew 25:21; emphasis added). Notice it doesn't say "good and *successful* servant" or "good and *perfect* servant." Just *faithful*. But what does being faithful mean? In a women's leadership group at my church, we discussed the journeys of scriptural giants such as Moses and Mary. Their journeys were definitely not easy. Moses wandered the desert for forty years and wasn't allowed to enter the Holy Land. Mary experienced humiliation and judgment for being pregnant before she was married and then watched her son die on a cross. Their journeys were incredibly difficult, yet God blessed their faithfulness. When I look at a story like Grayson and Leslie's, I think the same thing: the journey is not easy, yet God blesses our faithfulness.

THE CHRISTIAN CALL TO CARE FOR VULNERABLE CHILDREN

Christians are strong supporters of adoption and foster care, and they adopt and foster at a higher rate than the general population. A survey from the Barna Group (2013) found that 5 percent of practicing Christians have adopted, compared to 2 percent of all Americans. Similarly, 38 percent of practicing Christians have seriously considered adoption, compared to 26 percent of all Americans. In regard to foster care, the pattern of findings is similar. Three percent of practicing Christians have fostered, compared to 2 percent of all Americans; 31 percent of practicing Christians have seriously considered fostering, compared to 11 percent of all Americans.

Why do Christians adopt and foster children at a higher rate than the general population? Part of the reason may relate to Christianity's strong emphasis on caring for vulnerable children. In Christian adoption circles we often talk about James 1:27, which says, "Care for widows and orphans in their time of distress." Even though not every child who enters foster care or who is adopted privately or internationally is an orphan by definition, the value of looking after a child in need relates to many situations. This emphasis on caring for vulnerable children who are adopted or in foster care is deeply connected to serving and giving, two primary core Christian values. In what follows, we'll walk through some of these core values. See if you can connect with them as you reflect on your own motivations to adopt or foster.

The Deep Inherent Worth and Value of All Humans

Foundational in the call to care for vulnerable children is the Christian emphasis on the deep inherent worth and value of all human beings. This inherent value is found in the very first chapter of the Bible, where we read that God created humans in his own image: "So God created mankind in his own image, in the image of God he created them; male and female he created them" (Genesis 1:27). This concept is called the *imago dei*, and it is one of the elements of Christian spirituality. All human beings are created in the image of

God, irrespective of their race, ethnicity, nationality, gender, ability or disability status, or socioeconomic status. Regardless of one's background or status, everyone is made in the image of God. Period. Because of this deep truth, every person has worth and value, and no one can take that away from them.

This principle is also linked with the concept of grace that we see throughout the Bible. God doesn't love us because of our status or the things that we do for him. We don't earn our way to God through our actions or good behavior. That's how the world works. Instead, God loves us regardless of our actions or status. In fact, the Christian message says that God loves us even though we are sinners and do bad things. We are saved not by our status or the things we do, but rather we are saved by grace: "For it is by grace you have been saved, through faith—and this is not from yourselves, it is the gift of God—not by works, so that no one can boast" (Ephesians 2:8–9).

The idea that all human beings have deep inherent worth to God is incredibly motivating to the call of caring for vulnerable children, who are often forgotten in our society and world. At times they are literally abandoned by their first families (whose job was to care for them), abused or neglected, or orphaned because their parents are deceased. Vulnerable children are unable to take care of themselves. They are often viewed as "less than" because of their status or situation; people may choose not to value their voice or treat them like human beings, but discard them like pieces of trash. This action breaks God's heart. God sees vulnerable children as precious children of deep value. He loves and cares for them just as much as he loves and cares for you and me. The same is true for birth families. If we want to follow God in our lives, our hearts need to break for the things that break God's heart. We need to view vulnerable children and vulnerable families in the same way God does—as human beings who have deep value, worth, and preciousness.

Love and Mercy

Perhaps the most important core values seen throughout all of scripture are love and mercy. When the Pharisees asked Jesus what the greatest commandment in the Law was, Jesus said, "Love the Lord your God with all your heart and with all your soul and with all your mind. This is the first and greatest commandment. And the second is like it: Love your neighbor as yourself. All the Law and the Prophets hang on these two commandments" (Matthew 22:37–40). Love God and love others. It's simple, but incredibly hard to do.

Even in Jesus's day, the people who followed him had a tough time figuring out what it meant to love your neighbor. Following a discussion about the greatest commandment to love God and love one's neighbor, one expert in the law asked, "And who is my neighbor?" (Luke 10:29). In our own lives, we might ask the same thing. How far does this "love thing" have to go?

Jesus answered how he often did, with a story:

> "A man was going down from Jerusalem to Jericho, when he was attacked by robbers. They stripped him of his clothes, beat him and went away, leaving him half dead. A priest happened to be going down the same road, and when he saw the man, he passed by on the other side. So too, a Levite, when he came to the place and saw him, passed by on the other side. But a Samaritan, as he traveled, came where the man was; and when he saw him, he took pity on him. He went to them and bandaged his wounds, pouring on oil and wine. Then he put the man on his donkey, brought him to an inn and took care of him. The next day he took out two denarii and gave them to the innkeeper. 'Look after him,' he said, 'and when I return, I will reimburse you for any extra expense you may have.'

"Which of these three do you think was a neighbor to the man who fell into the hands of robbers?"

The expert in the law replied, "The one who had mercy on him."

Jesus told him, "Go and do likewise."

Luke 10:30–37

There are two key takeaways from this story. First, the command to love your neighbor doesn't just refer to people who are part of your group. The Jews and Samaritans hated each other; that's why it was so shocking that Jesus used a Samaritan as the hero in his story. This is a key point in God's call to love vulnerable children. Caring for those who are part of our biological family is natural. We are connected to them by blood. Pretty much everyone cares for their biological families, even animals. But as Christians, we are called to care for those who are not part of our group—people outside our biological family, vulnerable children, the fatherless—and to love them as our own.

Second, love is more than just having positive feelings toward someone. Love is tangible and gritty. In our culture today, we often think about love as a positive feeling. We fall in love. I love the Toronto Maple Leafs. My husband, Josh, loves *Star Wars*. But the Christian call to love is something entirely different. The Good Samaritan didn't just love with his feelings—he loved with time, energy, sweat, and money. He loved with his actions and resources. Too often Christians say they love and care for vulnerable children, but they really mean that they feel positively toward or think it's a good idea to support vulnerable children. But loving vulnerable children as Jesus commanded means to love with our time, energy, actions, and resources. It's being the hands and feet of Jesus. Imagine loving the way Christ loves us. Jesus was nailed to a cross and the people he loved hurled insults at him and demanded he be crucified, yet he still loves us.

Justice

Justice was a big deal in the Bible. For example, in the Old Testament, the Israelites were commanded to prioritize justice for the needy and the oppressed: "For the LORD your God is God of gods and Lord of lords, the great God, mighty and awesome, who shows no partiality and accepts no bribes. He defends the cause of the fatherless and widow, and loves the foreigner residing among you, giving them food and clothing. And you are to love those who are foreigners, for you yourselves were foreigners in Egypt" (Deuteronomy 10:17–19).

In a similar way, there was a special place in Jesus' heart for those in society who were needy and oppressed. Jesus tells a story in which the righteous get to heaven and meet with God face-to-face:

> "Then the King will say to those on his right, 'Come, you who are blessed by my Father; take your inheritance, the kingdom prepared for you since the creation of the world. For I was hungry and you gave me something to eat, I was thirsty and you gave me something to drink, I was a stranger and you invited me in, I needed clothes and you clothed me, I was sick and you looked after me, I was in prison and you came to visit me.'
>
> "Then the righteous will answer him, 'Lord, when did we see you hungry and feed you, or thirsty and give you something to drink? When did we see you a stranger and invite you in, or needing clothes and clothe you? When did we see you sick or in prison and go visit you?'
>
> "The King will reply, 'Truly I tell you, whatever you did

for one of the least of these brothers and sisters of mine, you did for me.'"

Matthew 25:34–40

This is incredible. Jesus is literally saying that when we care for the needy and oppressed—when we give them something to eat and drink, when we invite them into our home, and when we clothe them (in other words, when we care for vulnerable children)—we do this for God himself. Vulnerable children—those who grow up without families of their own—are perhaps the neediest and most oppressed group of people on the planet. For many vulnerable children, their basic needs for food, water, and shelter are not met. Many vulnerable children grow up in unsafe environments, not receiving a foundation of love and attachment, so they struggle to move forward and form trusting relationships with others. God's heart breaks for the injustices that these children face. He is 100 percent about working for justice for the needy and oppressed, and if we want to be in line with God's heart, we need to be about justice also.

Faithfulness

The Bible is an amazing story of how God relates to his people over thousands of years. What amazes me most is God's faithfulness. Time after time, we screw up, but God finds a way to maintain relationship with us. We see this faithfulness in the beginning, with God's relationship with Adam and Eve. Even though Adam and Eve sinned and got off track, God still stuck with them, clothing them with animal skins and providing a way forward for Adam and Eve to continue to work and start a family (Genesis 3:21).

God's faithfulness is perhaps most concretely shown in the Old Testament through his covenant with Abram. A covenant is a serious promise, a solemn pact. In the Old Testament, God promises

Abram that he will make a great nation from his descendants: "Look up at the sky and count the stars—if indeed you can count them. . . . So shall your offspring be" (Genesis 15:5). Two chapters later, God elaborates,

> "As for me, this is my covenant with you: You will be the father of many nations. No longer will you be called Abram; your name will be Abraham, for I have made you a father of many nations. I will make you fruitful; I will make nations of you, and kings will come from you. I will establish my covenant as an everlasting covenant between me and you and your descendants after you for the generations to come, to be your God and the God of your descendants after you."
>
> *Genesis 17:4–7*

Throughout the Old Testament, the Israelites go back and forth between following God and going their own way. God sticks with his people through the ups and downs, even sending his own son Jesus to live, be an example to us, and die on our behalf: to redeem us. God's stance toward us is one of faithfulness, regardless of how far we have strayed. That part doesn't matter; *God is still for us.*

This value of faithfulness is a good model for us as we enter into adoption and foster care. Sometimes just surviving is a struggle, with the feeling that things will never improve. But just as God is faithful toward us, we have the opportunity to practice faithfulness toward the beautiful children who are in our care by sticking with them through the ups and downs, and loving them sacrificially. Through the many ups and downs, we can exercise faithfulness toward God, each other, and our families. I am confident that one day he will say to you, "Well done, good and *faithful* servant."

Adoption Mirrors God's Relationship with Us

One aspect of adoption and foster care that is incredibly beautiful is that it mirrors God's relationship with us. Because of our sin, the Bible says that we were separated from God. Our relationship with God was broken, leaving us in big trouble. But because God loved us, he sent his son, Jesus, so that we could be reconciled to him. The core message of Christianity is about that reconciliation and redemption. We can be reconciled with God, and the broken things can be made right again.

This perspective also speaks volumes to our children's journey. We can often feel as though their current behavior defines their future. We feel this way because our daily interactions with them can leave us exhausted and dismayed. We also see our children's frustration with how things are going. The combination can lead to hopelessness. But because of grace, no one need be hopeless, including our kids.

Adoption and reconciliation with God have certain parallels. Paul, in fact, explicitly uses adoption language to describe our reconciled relationship with God: "For those who are led by the Spirit of God are the children of God. The Spirit you received does not make you slaves, so that you live in fear again; rather, the Spirit you received brought about your adoption to sonship. And by him we cry, '*Abba*, Father.' The Spirit himself testifies with our spirit that we are God's children" (Romans 8:14–16). What a beautiful illustration of the Christian message! We are reconciled to God not as slaves but as sons and daughters. We are adopted. And if you decide to engage in adoption or foster care, know that you are engaging in deep, holy work that is close to the heart of God.

WISDOM AND DISCERNMENT

Christians can be incredibly motivated to care for vulnerable children, and I would never want to dissuade someone from pursuing it, especially if they feel God's call. At the same time, adopting and fostering require wisdom and discernment. In the Bible, wisdom and discernment are repeatedly presented as good things; the entire book of Proverbs is devoted to their importance. As Christians, we need to engage every part of our lives with wisdom and discernment. Caring for vulnerable children is no exception.

Wisdom involves the correct application of knowledge: the integration of knowledge and experience that comes over time. Whereas knowledge helps us figure out what is correct or true, wisdom helps us figure out how to apply that knowledge to our life. Wisdom often comes into play in the context of decision making.

Wisdom is also closely related to the process of discernment, which involves right judgment between alternatives, choices, and directions. Christians are called to "not treat prophecies with contempt but test them all; hold on to what is good, reject every kind of evil" (1 Thessalonians 5:20–22). Similarly, we are to "not believe every spirit, but test the spirits to see whether they are from God, because many false prophets have gone out into the world" (1 John 4:1).

Because vulnerable children's needs are so great, and the desire to love and care for children is so deep, we can feel emotionally compelled to take action, sometimes letting wisdom and discernment take a backseat. Maybe you've heard a pastor offer a compelling sermon about the number of orphans in the world looking for their forever family. I heard a pastor preach, "If every Christian family in the US adopted one child, we would have no more orphan crisis." Hearing a call like this, we might get caught up in our feelings and emotions, and subsequently pursue a course of action that doesn't set up our family for health and can negatively impact the very children we are trying to care for.

Certainly, everyone would welcome the end of the world's orphan crisis by placing every child in a safe and loving family. But we must exercise wisdom and discernment as we step forward, because it can be easy to mix up our own emotions with what God actually wants for us. Negative consequences occur when families rush headlong into adoption or foster care in a way that is not wise, balanced, or disciplined. Families struggle, marriages break up, placements fail, and kids return to the foster system. I've watched many kids bounce from home to home in foster care. When you are involved in supporting and loving vulnerable children, you want to be there for the long haul, pursuing love, mercy, justice, and faithfulness all along the way.

Think about the instructions you hear on an airplane: "Put your oxygen mask on first, before helping the person next to you," even if the person sitting next to you needs assistance. Why? Because if you haven't taken care of your own oxygen mask, you will soon be gasping for air yourself and in no position to help anyone else. More than reading this as a caution, I want to encourage you to read this as permission and encouragement to exercise wisdom and discernment. It is heartbreaking when we walk alongside families who entered the journey in an unbalanced way and now feel like they are way in over their heads.

But what important aspects should we consider before committing to adopt or foster? Many Christians might agree that wisdom and discernment are important, but figuring out what that process looks like can be difficult, especially if you are new to the adoption and foster care world. In the next section, I walk you through a step-by-step process of wisdom and discernment.

The Wisdom and Discernment Process

I recommend that families go through a five-part process when thinking about embarking on adoption or foster care. Families should engage this process from the outset, when they are even just considering adopting or fostering. Families should also take these steps when considering making a change in their adoption or foster care status, such as bringing an additional child into the home.

1. Involve All Family Members

The decision to adopt or foster affects the entire family: both of the parents and all the children living at home. In some situations, one spouse or family member is excited about adopting or fostering, but the other or others, not so much. In this case, one family member might move ahead with an agenda without involving the other family members.

Perhaps you can relate. Some of you may never have imagined adopting or fostering and are apprehensive about it, but your spouse really wants you to take the next step in considering it. Maybe, on the other hand, you feel a deep call and passion around adoption and foster care, and you wish your spouse's level of enthusiasm matched your own.

Engaging in this discernment process without other family members sets you up for problems later. Involve all family members in the process and give all family members time and space for their own discernment process. Unity between husband and wife is crucial when moving forward with a placement. In some cases, though, one spouse's desire to say yes to a placement is fueled by so much emotion that the person might inadvertently use Christian manipulation to convince the spouse to say yes. Then, when a child's emotions and behaviors become unmanageable and stress skyrockets, resentment and bitterness can divide spouses. God doesn't grow families to divide them. For a decision as important as adopting or fostering, everyone needs to be on board, and the best way to get there is to include everyone in the discernment process from the beginning.

This emphasis on inclusion refers to children as well as parents. Some parents think their kids are too young or immature to talk about these issues and be part of the family's discernment process. Maybe the parents don't want to get their kids' hopes up about adoption or foster care, in case the family ultimately decides not to do it. As a result, kids might be left in the dark until parents settle on the final decision. This big mistake can cause resentment and feelings of isolation in children who are a part of your home. Children are greatly affected when another child comes into the home through foster care or adoption; the children need to be part of the process from the very beginning.

Parents, welcome the opportunity to invite your children into this journey with you. Be models for them. Create the blueprint in their lives showing them that kids' voices matter, and that you have a deep commitment to working through things together as a family. Children may have valid questions or concerns that you should address prior to making any decision. Respond throughout the discernment process in open, developmentally appropriate conversations as an entire family. How this conversation plays out depends on your children's ages and maturity levels. With younger children, using play to communicate about the potential placement can be helpful; for example, demonstrate the changes that will take place in the family using dolls and dollhouses.

A licensed foster family I worked with was considering a placement of two boys, ages ten and five. The foster family invited me over to their home, and we sat around the dinner table with all five of their children, ranging in age between two and ten years old. The parents told me that they make decisions together as a family and that they wanted their children to be part of the placement conversation. The children and parents asked me many questions, and we were able to have the discussion all together.

Another foster mom, Jamie Finn, shared that her four-year-old daughter said this about a newborn placement: "I wish we could adopt her, but she has a mommy. She's my sister now, but when her mommy's ready, she'll get to be with her again." She's four and already gets it! Jamie expressed these words of encouragement: "Speak to your kids about foster care the way you hope they will think about foster care, because they're listening. And live out foster care the way you hope they'll live out foster care, because they're watching."

2. Invite Your Community

Other family members, close friends, and members of one's church community are all great candidates to involve in the discernment process. First, *invite people who have your best interests at heart*. You don't want people in this process who are not for you and your family. Folks who don't understand why you are choosing to do this or who are judgmental are the last people you want at this time as part of your community or inner circle of trusted friends or family members.

Second, *invite people who have knowledge and experience with adoption and foster care*, and who can give you informed feedback about this journey. Education and community go hand in hand.

Third, *give people permission to share their opinions or impressions freely*. Sometimes we might think we want the opinions of others, but really we just want people to confirm the direction we already desire. This is called *confirmation bias* (Nickerson, 1998) and is not likely to be helpful. Groups can also become engaged in *groupthink* (Janis, 1971), in which members tend to resist bringing up contradictory opinions. To combat confirmation bias and groupthink, surround yourselves with a variety of people and perspectives and explicitly invite them to express their opinion, even—or perhaps especially— if it differs from your own or the group's dominant stance.

We also strongly encourage families to join an adoption and foster care support group if one is available in their area. Support groups can be immensely helpful in gaining an eyes-wide-open experience in your discernment journey. You will also be surrounded by support from the outset, which can be a game changer.

3. Seek God's Guidance

I love the Wesleyan tradition's acknowledging of four sources of truth: scripture, Christian tradition, experience, and reason. I believe God works through each of these areas, and a thorough seeking of God's guidance will include consideration of each source. For Christ-followers, *scripture* is an invaluable source of God's message. Families should be diligent about searching the scriptures to seek what God would have them do regarding caring for vulnerable children. Understand how the history of the *Christian tradition* of caring for vulnerable children sets the stage for how we do so today. Our personal *experience* of God through prayer can be a source of wisdom and direction. Finally, incorporate *reason*, research, and known best practices. To begin your education along these lines, blogs, public forums, Facebook groups, and websites can provide insight and wisdom. Online research can be especially overwhelming if you don't know a few pointers, so I've provided a list of helpful resources in the appendices.

4. Assess Your Family

I encourage families considering adoption or foster care to meet with a trained therapist knowledgeable in this area to discuss any issues and get feedback. At a minimum, a family assessment should pose the following questions:

- What is each family member's mental and physical health status? Do any significant issues need to be addressed before beginning the adoption or foster care journey?
- What is the status of the parents' marriage relationship (if

applicable)? Is the marriage healthy and vibrant? Do any issues or problems need resolution before beginning this journey?

- What is the family's current level of stress? If it's high, dealing with the existing stressors first might be a better step before adding another individual to the family system.
- What is the family's current level of support? Are the parents and children integrated into a community that can help with their emotional and tangible needs? Are other family members, friends, and the church involved? Does the family have sources of support that are familiar with adoption and foster care? How informed is the church community about adoption and fostering issues?

If as a family you recognize that some issues should be addressed first, that's not necessarily an indication that God doesn't want you to adopt or foster. Perhaps some more groundwork and preparation need to be done first. For example, if you are dealing with an unresolved marital issue right now, consider pressing pause on adoption and fostering and enter into a season of marriage counseling. Once that marital issue is in a better place, you could reengage with the adoption or foster discernment process.

5. Take Your Time

Families can get really excited about adoption and foster care and rush the process, or they feel a sense of urgency because so many children are in need. Hurrying is a problem. When you rush the process, you may not consider all the important factors in your decision, especially if you are experiencing a big push of emotions or feelings. Feelings come and go, and it's important to wait a bit for strong feelings to fade, to see if the decision still seems wise when the tides have shifted. Take your time. This important decision will strongly affect the lives of you, your family members, and the possible children coming into your care. You will not be adequately prepared for everything you'll encounter, but taking the time necessary to plan, prepare, and gain insights gives you a massive head start.

In all areas of life, there is a wise progression of development. You don't train for a marathon by running twenty-six miles the first day. Along these lines, many families try to do too much too soon when it comes to adoption and foster care. For example, after deciding to adopt, a couple gets a call about a group of four siblings who want to stay together. The couple is pulled in that direction, and all of a sudden they have gone from zero children in the home to four adopted brothers. Remember, many times our kiddos have trauma histories that carry with them emotional and behavioral challenges. Few families are prepared for that kind of sudden increase in load and stress. Whereas adopting one child might be okay, four at once can more likely result in a failed placement or a marriage in tatters. It's okay to take into consideration your bandwidth when deciding to say yes or no to a placement. When engaging in adoption and foster care, don't take on too much too soon. Take one small step at a time, becoming accustomed as a family to that step. Once the family reaches equilibrium and homeostasis, you can decide to take another step or to stay where you are.

My friend Andrew Schneidler describes the family system as a canoe traveling down a river. Deciding to adopt a child or accept a foster placement is like adding a child into your canoe who is struggling in the water. Feeling compelled to rescue children is a good motivation. If you add a manageable load, you will be able to navigate down the river and stay afloat. But if you add more passengers than you are capable of supporting, the risk is that the canoe will start to take on water or even capsize. As with the airplane's oxygen mask, you can't help your children if you are struggling to stay afloat yourself. Evaluate your level of resources and support, and don't capsize your canoe.

Leslie and Grayson took the wisdom and discernment process seriously. They spent hours discussing how God might want them to grow their family. If they were going to adopt, they wanted to make sure both were on the same page and hearing similarly from God. They also were serious about seeking God's guidance. The couple didn't want to make this decision alone; they were disciplined about their prayers, and they invited their community to pray for God's guidance as well. Grayson and Leslie also took their time, not wanting to rush such an important decision. This process of wisdom and discernment was invaluable for them. Their community helped them seek God's heart and also asked them tough questions about their motivations. Grayson remembers his pastor asking him to commit to seeking God in prayer every day for a month. What did he hear God telling him about moving forward with the adoption? What was he hearing from God through the scriptures? Was Grayson at all motivated to adopt because of pride or the need for others to see him as a great Christian? These were tough questions to answer, but by the time they moved forward with their adoption journey, Grayson and Leslie were confident that they had put in the time to seek God's heart for their family.

What Does God Promise Us?

Christian families who adopt or foster often feel a strong call from God to enter this journey. They often have a huge passion for loving and caring for children and a longing for them to be part of a safe and healthy family. Stepping forward often means making huge sacrifices—giving of their time and finances, taking on additional stress—to bring children into their home.

Then the problems mount. Some children may have difficulties attaching to the parents, and the normal positive reinforcement that parents usually expect (hugs, snuggles, "I love yous") may not happen. The marriage relationship may hit a rough patch because of all the added strain, and single parents may get exhausted because they have to be "on" 100 percent of the time. Feelings of grief, anger, and disappointment can emerge because what they hoped their family would be like (e.g., affectionate) is far from their reality.

These experiences can disrupt one's relationship with God, which is normal. We all go through fluctuations over time in how we experience God. But this particular struggle is exacerbated by a deep misunderstanding of God and what God promises us, and ultimately relates to the origin of religion itself.

In ancient times, religions developed to explain phenomena outside of human control (Bell, 2008). For example, farmers noticed that sometimes the rain would be plentiful and their crops would produce enough food to support their community. Other times, the rain would disappear, the sun would scorch the crops, and people in the community would starve to death. The community couldn't explain what was happening, so they believed that gods controlled natural phenomena like the sun and rain. Communities developed complex sacrificial systems to obtain the favor of their gods, sometimes going as far as sacrificing their own children. This sort of thinking seems ancient, but we continue today to deal with the underlying message: *If I [fill in the blank], then I will receive God's favor and things will turn out well for me.*

This dynamic is present in the older brother's perspective in the parable of the Prodigal Son (Luke 15:11–31). In this story, a father has two sons. The younger brother asks for his inheritance early, goes off to a foreign land, and wastes all of his dad's money on wild living. The older brother stays back and works diligently the whole time. The younger son becomes destitute, comes to his senses, and returns home humbly. The father is so overjoyed that his younger son has returned that he throws a big party for him. The older son refuses to go inside and join in the celebration, indignant at the lack of fairness of the whole thing.

The older brother is steeped in a "just world" way of thinking (Lerner, 1980). In that mode, people get what they deserve. Good things happen to good people, and bad things happen to bad people. The older brother was good, so he should reap the benefits. Seeing the younger brother reap the benefits (the party, the fattened calf) even though he engaged in bad behavior was infuriating. He doesn't understand the father's outlook that "you are always with me, and everything I have is yours" (Luke 15:31). The older brother believes he is getting a raw deal.

This line of thinking can happen to all Christians but is especially common in adoptive and foster families. Families feel as if they are following what God wants for their life and are making huge sacrifices to obey. Both parts of that statement are typically accurate.

But then they make the mistake of the older brother in the parable. They assume that *because of their faithfulness and sacrifices, God should reward them by making everything work out.* I certainly am guilty of this mind-set. Usually we have some set of predetermined beliefs about what it means for everything to work out, such as well-behaved children who love and appreciate their parents for the sacrifices made. When reality falls short of expectations, the feeling is that God has broken his promise. Like the older brother, people feel like they've gotten a raw deal.

Grayson and Leslie often felt this way. They were so connected with God and their church community, spending such an intensive time on wisdom and discernment, that they were absolutely confident that adoption was what God wanted them to do. They probably wouldn't have said this out loud, but they both had the belief that if they followed what God wanted for their life, things would work out: their kids would develop normally, do well in school, and love and appreciate Grayson and Leslie as parents. When their kids struggled, the couple began to get frustrated and even doubt God. Things were not working out as they had expected, so they began to question whether they had heard God correctly in the first place.

But what does God ultimately promise us? He never promises that life will be easy or comfortable. In fact, Jesus actually seems to promise the opposite. "In this world you will have trouble" (John 16:33a). Jesus said that his followers would be persecuted as he had been persecuted (John 15:20), and that the world would hate them (John 15:18–19). Even Jesus lamented and felt deep sorrow. Before he died, Jesus cried out to God, "My God, my God, why have you forsaken me?" (Matthew 27:46). We might be uncomfortable with Jesus expressing deep sorrow, but it was an honest part of his experience. If Jesus can cry out to God, "Where are you?" and "Why is this happening?" perhaps this can say something to us. Struggle and lament are important aspects of our human experience. We are not promised a life without challenges.

So . . . what *can* we count on God for? *God promises to be with us in the midst of our struggles and difficulties.* Jesus promises us trouble in this world (John 16:33a), but thankfully he doesn't leave us there alone. He continues by saying, "But take heart! I have overcome the world" (John 16:33b). Paul writes that he is "convinced that neither death nor life, neither angels nor demons, neither the present nor the future, nor any powers, neither height nor depth, nor anything else in all creation, will be able to separate us from the love of God that is in Christ Jesus our Lord" (Romans 8:38–39). That's a pretty comprehensive list, and the message is clear. God is with us through everything—the highs and lows, good and bad times, and successes and failures. We aren't promised an easy journey; we are promised that the God who has overcome the world will be with us every step of the way.

EXERCISE: PROCESS OF WISDOM AND DISCERNMENT

Consider where you are right now in the process of wisdom and discernment around adoption and foster care. For what are you seeking God's direction?

_____

_____

_____

_____

_____

_____

To what extent have you included the whole family, your spouse and children, in this discernment process? What is one step you could take to include the entire family in this journey?

_____

_____

_____

_____

_____

_____

_____

To what extent have you invited your community along with you on this process of discernment? How could you include other family members, friends, and your church community in this process? Have you invited anyone to speak to you who has experience with adoption and foster care? How could you invite your community to be honest with you, even if they have feedback that would be difficult for you to hear?

_____

_____

_____

_____

_____

_____

_____

To what extent have you invited God into your process of discernment? In seeking God's guidance through scripture, church tradition, personal experience (e.g., prayer), and reason, what do you hear God saying to you?

_____

_____

_____

_____

_____

_____

Assess where your family is right now in regard to the following areas:

Mental and physical health:

_____

_____

_____

Marriage relationship (if applicable):

_____

_____

_____

Current stress level:

_____

_____

_____

Current support level:

_____

_____

_____

Remember this key point: take your time in the wisdom and discernment process. Are there any factors right now that are rushing your decision? Are you feeling any pressure to make a decision quickly? How could you slow down the process to ensure that you are diligent in your process of wisdom and discernment?

_____

_____

_____

_____

_____

_____

Remember the suggestion to start small and move slowly. If you feel as if God is leading you to take a step forward in this area, what would it look like for your family to take a small step forward? Is anything in your life urging you to take a huge step forward? What would it look like to take a small step and then reassess the situation?

_____

_____

_____

_____

_____

SECTION 2

The Replanted Model

CHAPTER 4

The Soil
Emotional Support

Many people need desperately to receive this message:
"I feel and think much as you do, care about many of the things
you care about, although most people do not care
about them. You are not alone."

—KURT VONNEGUT JR.

I N PREVIOUS CHAPTERS I discussed ways to reduce or manage
the stress in our lives, but in these next few chapters I'm going to
address the other side of the equation: how can we work to build the
necessary resources and support to navigate the journey of adoption
and foster care in a way that promotes healing, growth, and vibrancy?

Based on my work with adoptive and foster families, the Replanted
model is built on three key sources of support (Groze, 1996): emotional support, informational support, and tangible support. Every
day children impacted by adoption or foster care are being replanted
in a new garden, represented by their new adoptive or foster family,
whether permanently or temporarily. The theme verse for this book
and ministry is from Isaiah 61:3b: "They will be called oaks of righteousness, a planting of the LORD for the display of his splendor."

For adoptive and foster families to grow and thrive, and for
our precious kids to be replanted in a way that leads to healing
and growth, you need three key types of support. First, you need
emotional support—the good soil. Parents and children need deep,
grace-filled relationships with other people who really understand

where they are coming from. Families need to know and experience, deep in their collective soul, that they are not alone. Second, you need *informational support*—the sunlight. Many adoptive and foster families face unique challenges raising their children, and getting trained and educated is essential. Third, you need *tangible support*—the water. It may sound simple, but if you don't have the practical support you need around food, supplies, toys, babysitting, and other basic needs, nothing else is going to matter. Basic needs must be met in order to set a foundation for a healthy family.

In this chapter, we tackle emotional support, the good soil. It's one thing to be told, "You are not alone" or "We are in your corner," but personally feeling or experiencing the truth of these statements is an entirely different matter. On the adoptive and foster journey, parents go through a lot of deep-seated emotions: loss, grief, fear, anxiety, stress, and more. Parents can learn all about trauma and how to better handle children in the face of extreme behaviors, and parents can also discover strategies for connecting with an emotionally detached child. All of that is extremely helpful and can even be healing to some degree. But to have another person offer true empathy is restorative. In her book *Braving the Wilderness*, Brené Brown (2017) talks about a common theme in bluegrass music called the high lonesome. It's a guttural emotion that pours out from deep feeling, deep loss, or deep grief, which many of us experience at some point. What makes the high lonesome so powerful in bluegrass is that it's a shared experience; it's never meant to be experienced alone. And when you share in the high lonesome with another human being, there is healing. The pain may not go away and your struggle may not diminish, but you are now sharing it with someone else—another flesh-and-blood human being who is limping through this broken life just like you. That shared experience is exactly what families need in order to find a place of healing on this journey.

JOSEPH AND SALLIE

Joseph and Sallie were a white couple who had been married ten years, were committed Christians, and had two children—Grace (age seven) and Lilly (age four). They wanted a larger family but also had a heart for caring for vulnerable children that was rooted in their Christian commitment. They began to learn about adoption and foster care, prayerfully considering whether God might have them enter this journey as a family.

They decided to do foster care and went through the process of preparing their home. They also went through the interview process, were approved, and were asked if they could take in a five-year-old boy named Jerrod. Jerrod was an African American child who was put into the system about a year before. His mother had been abusing substances, and her boyfriend had been physically abusing Jerrod while she was at work.

Jerrod was a sweet boy who was very energetic and active. He loved basketball and it was difficult to get him to change out of his little LeBron James jersey. He enjoyed laughing and being goofy, and he would entertain the family for hours by telling the same knock-knock joke over and over, and making funny faces at Grace and Lilly. He had a caring heart and was often cuddly and affectionate with Joseph and Sallie. They loved having Jerrod as part of their family.

At the same time, the transition into foster care was difficult for Jerrod. He missed his mother and was only able to see her for supervised visits one time per week for an hour. As a result of his trauma experiences, he had a hard time regulating his emotions. He would sometimes lash out in anger, screaming at Joseph and Sallie when he wouldn't get his way or was told no. When he was upset, sometimes he would throw or intentionally break things in the home; other times he would become physically aggressive, flailing his arms at Joseph and Sallie when they confronted him. He was sad he couldn't be with his mother. He missed his community and friends. At his new school, none of the kids looked like him. They were mostly white. He felt like he didn't fit in, uprooted and forced to navigate an unfamiliar environment. He felt alone and unknown.

Grace and Lilly also had a hard time with the transition. Although they were excited about welcoming a new brother into the home, connecting with Jerrod was challenging for them. Not long after Jerrod came into the home, Lilly started asking her mom if they could "give Jerrod back." One time Lilly voiced this out loud in front of Jerrod. Sallie tried to shush Lilly right away but it was too late, and Jerrod ran up to his bedroom and slammed the door. Jerrod hadn't been physically aggressive with the girls to that point, but Joseph and Sallie were nervous about it, so they were vigilant in watching over the kids at all times.

Joseph and Sallie cared for Jerrod for almost two years when the transition plan was developed to have Jerrod return to his birth mother. The family loved him deeply, and they had developed a close bond with one another. The frequency and duration of visits home began to increase, and then periodic overnight visits became part of the routine. The reality of Jerrod returning home was tangible. With each visit, Joseph's and Sallie's hearts broke a little more. He was their son too, and this had been his home for a long time. The girls were also having a hard time understanding that Jerrod would not be living with them anymore. They asked if they would still see him after he left. How could he just leave?

Over the course of their fostering, Joseph and Sallie's challenges were exacerbated because they didn't feel like they had anyone who understood and supported them. They thought they had a good group of friends, but once they fostered Jerrod, the couple's perspective shifted. They noticed that most of their friends didn't really know how to deal with situations involving deep pain and broken-ness. Of course, they all had their own problems, which they seemed to pretty much deal with on their own. If their friends shared their struggles with each other, it was kind of a give-and-take, almost with its own rhythm and standards. Joseph and Sallie realized that, in their group of friends, an unconscious rule was that you shouldn't burden each other too much. The message seemed to be: if you were going through a difficult time, that's okay, but make sure it doesn't last too long, and next time you can repay the support to the other person.

The problem was that Joseph and Sallie were in a tough spot and resolution didn't seem in sight. Their friends were supportive at first, but Joseph and Sallie could tell they were a bit overwhelmed by the couple's situation. At first, they would try to be helpful and give advice, but when their advice didn't work right away, the friends didn't really know what to do. Many of their friends didn't know how to navigate being a transracial family or how important it was to keep Jerrod connected to his cultural background. Just being with Sallie and Joseph in their situation seemed to make them anxious.

Other friends and family members would be openly critical with the way Joseph and Sallie were running their family. The couple had learned that punitive discipline and consequence-oriented tech-niques, like spanking or time-outs, were less likely to be effective for children with a history of trauma, but they had trouble controlling Jerrod's behavior. He would get too aggressive when playing with other children (pushing or shoving), and some of the other moms would get angry. Through the grapevine, Sallie even heard that some of her friends had criticized her parenting, calling her "permissive" and wondering if that was part of the reason Jerrod's behavior was so poor. Joseph and Sallie began to feel like they were on their own. Their family was struggling, and the isolation and lack of support made it feel much worse.

When Jerrod returned to his biological mother, Joseph and Sallie both experienced tremendous grief and even felt depressed for quite some time. Cognitively, they knew it was good for Jerrod to be reunited with his mother. They were happy she experienced healing and could be the mother Jerrod needed her to be. They had been cheering for her all this time. But, deep down, if they were completely honest with themselves, sometimes they wished she had failed so Jerrod could have been with them forever. It was hard to hold all those feelings. Their friends and family tried to be supportive, but their support seemed to come with an expiration date. Some friends didn't understand why Joseph and Sallie continued to have a hard time. Some people even expressed relief when Jerrod went home, as if the couple's problem had been fixed. These friends didn't understand how much Joseph and Sallie loved Jerrod, and how much they missed him.

Key Elements of Emotionally Supportive Relationships

Feeling alone and unsupported is one of the worst feelings people can experience. In fact, I think that being alone in your pain is about as close to hell as we can get on earth. It's a terrible feeling. We weren't meant to do life alone (Genesis 2:18). We need other people to go through life with us with an abundance of grace and love. We need other people to help pick us up when we fall down (Ecclesiastes 4:9–12).

But what does emotional support look like in reality? What kinds of relationships do we need? If you are an adoptive or foster parent, how should these relationships appear and feel? What qualities should we be seeking out in others with whom we want to develop relationships? If we are the church and we want to support adoptive and foster families, what kinds of people should we be striving to be?

Emotionally supportive relationships have several aspects. In what follows, I try to paint a picture of the elements of emotionally supportive relationships for which adoptive and foster families are typically longing. These elements are based on theory and research exploring how relationships and small groups can facilitate healing and growth and are the primary foundation for our Replanted groups (Hook, Hook, & Davis, 2017; Yalom, 1970).

As you read through the key elements of emotionally supportive relationships, think about your own relationships right now. If you are an adoptive or foster family, to what extent are your relationships characterized by grace, safety, vulnerability, and truth? Similarly, if you are an individual or church community with a goal of supporting adoptive and foster families, to what extent are you offering grace, safety, vulnerability, and truth to the families in your community?

Grace

Acceptance is one of our most important needs as human beings. The most painful times in your life probably have to do with rejection or not being accepted in some manner. At a deep, heart level, we all long to be accepted and part of the group. In most aspects of life, though, acceptance is conditional. If we are good, succeed, and play by the rules, we earn acceptance. On the other hand, if we are bad, fail, or miss the mark, we are rejected. It's tough and scary to be involved in relationships characterized by conditional acceptance.

Grace involves unconditional acceptance. Grace is based in our relationship with God, who loves and accepts us even though we miss the mark. Christianity teaches that we don't have to earn our way to God; instead, God reaches out to us first because of his love for us. In turn, because of the love we receive from God, we can extend grace to each other in our relationships here on earth. God's grace is sufficient.

Grace can be difficult for all of us, both giving and receiving it. Parents sometimes can have a tough time extending grace to themselves and each other. This road can be hard, especially when parenting a child with trauma. Parents often express how they feel like they've messed up, they are terrible parents, and they wish they knew then what they know now. But every parent should experience grace—the kind of grace that God gives to us so freely and beautifully, not because he has to but because he loves us so deeply. We also need to extend grace to our children, especially when they are having trouble. We should be delighting in our children, even in their hard seasons. They are always precious.

Adoptive and foster families often experience more judgment than grace, which is heartbreaking. This posture of judgment usually comes from a lack of understanding. Because giving and receiving grace are hard, having relationships characterized by grace is so incredibly important. We all need relationships where we can be loved and accepted right where we are, regardless of whatever is happening or how we are "performing" that day.

For example, Sallie began to develop a close friendship with a woman from church named Ruth. Ruth hadn't adopted or fostered herself, but she had been through tough times with her two biological children, so she was able to empathize with Sallie. One of Ruth's children had struggled off and on for years with drug addiction, so Ruth understood pain and the need for grace. Ruth didn't judge or criticize Sallie; instead, Ruth encouraged Sallie and gave her space to be authentic, even about her struggles. This relationship was healing for Sallie. She could be her real self and honest about her flaws and shortcomings.

Safety

Safety involves protection from danger. Physical and emotional safety are both important. Psychologist Abraham Maslow (1943) said that safety was one of our most foundational human needs. It is difficult to thrive, trust, and build relationships when we don't feel safe. A relationship that doesn't feel safe won't have the opportunity to grow. Safety can be thought of as a prerequisite for emotionally supportive relationships.

Think about your own relationships. What makes you feel safe with your closest friends? Maybe it is having a friend who consistently shows up, accepts you, prays with you, and strives to know your heart. Conversely, lots of things can derail safety. What makes you feel unsafe? Relationships can feel unsafe when they include criticism and judgment. When on the receiving end, you sense that you aren't doing a good job, you've messed up, and you are a failure. We can be quick to give advice because we want to fix problems. We want to make pain or difficulty go away. However, leading with advice instead of listening to parents unconditionally and empathetically can send the wrong message. Instead of criticizing or giving advice, let's just sit with families in their pain. Validate it. Feel what they feel. Ask them what support would be helpful. Thank them for sharing and follow up. Pray with them.

As part of their goal to develop more emotional support in their lives, Sallie and Joseph joined a support group of other adoptive and foster families. One helpful thing about the support group was the set of ground rules designed to keep the relationships safe. For example, one ground rule was that whatever was shared in group stayed in the group. Joseph and Sallie didn't have to worry about the people in their group sharing their personal stories, because everyone made a commitment to confidentiality. Another ground rule involved offering no judgments or criticism. The group leader knew how important safety was, so she made the group a judgment-free zone. Joseph and Sallie could share openly in the group without fear that other people would make fun of or look down on them.

Vulnerability

Vulnerability involves being open and honest about who you really are and how you are doing. An emotionally supportive relationship involves two people being open and vulnerable with each other. When two people's true, authentic selves meet, magic happens. It's as if you can breathe all of a sudden after holding your breath underwater for a long time.

Being vulnerable is a challenge. Most of us struggle to some extent with vulnerability. We might feel as if our authentic selves are too messy for others. We worry that if we let other people in and show them our true selves, wounds and all, people would be gone for good. We don't trust that we would be accepted just as we are. And we often want to protect our children in a similar way.

In response to our fear, we often hide and put on our masks. Hiding is a common response to brokenness and shame, rooted in the fall. After they sinned, Adam and Eve hid from God and each other. Adam and Eve had lived in open relationship with God. Adam walked with God in the cool of the garden, enjoying a sense of intimacy and connection. After they sinned, however, God had to call out for Adam and Eve and search for them. In a similar way, before the fall, Adam and Eve lived in open relationship with each other. They were "naked and not ashamed." But after they sinned, Adam and Eve realized that they were naked. They sewed fig leaves together to cover themselves. They hid.

This pattern of hiding continues today. We do it when we have problems. We might not leave the house for days at a time or visit with family or friends. We might not go to church. When someone asks how we are doing, we might say, "Fine, thank you," and change the subject. (When someone says they are fine, that often means, "Feelings Inside Not Expressed.")

Putting on masks involves assuming a particular persona. For example, we might wear the mask of "Superhero Mom" or "Loving,

Supportive Dad." This is who we want to be, so we take that mask and put it on. We pretend to be something we aren't in order to protect ourselves. It's a defense mechanism. Pretending might work for a while, but wearing masks kills vulnerability and real connection with others, who can only connect with the persona we are trying to portray. Emotionally supportive relationships are impossible when masks are in place.

The alternative is to take a risk, take off our masks, and try vulnerability. Vulnerability requires courage because you have to put forth your true, authentic self. Being vulnerable is scary because you could be rejected, and rejection may feel terrible because your true, authentic self is all that you have. Being rejected for who we are is terrifying, but taking the risk to be vulnerable can also result in a huge gain: if we are not rejected, if the person we are engaging with has grace and is safe, we have a chance to be affirmed and accepted as we truly are—what our soul deeply craves. Ann Voskamp summarized this idea perfectly at our recent conference, sharing that "shame dies when our stories are told in safe places." Amen!

Joseph and Sallie found it tough to be vulnerable when they first joined their small group. They were worried about what other members of the group would think of them if they were truly honest about their fears and doubts, especially some of their feelings of anger and fear toward their foster son, Jerrod. At first, they held back, not wanting to share too much. But eventually, as they observed the other group members sharing and learned that the group was safe, they took the risk to share more about themselves. They were willing to share parts of themselves that they weren't proud of. For example, Joseph shared about losing his temper and yelling at Jerrod. Sallie shared about her debilitating fear about Jerrod's uncertain future. Thankfully, when they shared, they received grace from the group. The other members nodded and said they had similar experiences. The group leaders, Natalie and Devin, encouraged them, noting how courageous they were to share their story. Little by little, as Joseph and Sallie shared more vulnerably, they felt more connected to the group and more supported in their journey. What a beautiful experience—to have friends who understand what you're going through and understand you can deeply love the son you are fostering and hold anger and fear all at the same time.

When Mike and Kristin Berry launched the Confessions of an Adoptive Parent blog, it was born out of an experience where they had joined with fellow adoptive parents who were parenting children from significant places of trauma. All of these families gathered together were struggling big-time. But sitting in that room and sharing openly without the fear of judgment was life-giving for them, especially for Mike and Kristin, who at the time were in a state of peril. One of their kids had held the family hostage with his extreme temper tantrums and aggression. To be with people who just nodded when Mike and Kristin confessed their deepest struggles was liberating. It birthed a global community.

Truth

As you develop relationships that are grace-filled, safe, and vulnerable, you provide a context where truth can be given and received. In healthy, emotionally supportive relationships, people are able to tell each other the truth, even when it is difficult. For example, you would be able to give feedback about something that was hurtful or draw an appropriate boundary. Also, emotionally supportive relationships involve growth and discipleship, and being honest with each other is essential for that process to happen.

In the Bible, Jesus connects truth with freedom. He says that if we follow him, we will know the truth, and the truth will set us free (John 8:32). So, there is something important about knowing the truth and being able to tell the truth to each other. It helps us experience freedom, healing, and growth. The Bible also says that Jesus was full of grace and truth (John 1:14). He wasn't one or the other, or the midpoint between grace and truth—he was both, fully. If we want to develop healthy, emotionally supportive relationships with others, we need those relationships to be characterized by both grace and truth as well.

Truth is sometimes difficult to give and receive, however. Sometimes truth can come across as criticism or judgment, which we already noted can make a relationship feel unsafe. The context in which truth is given is important. Paul writes that it is essential to speak the truth in love (Ephesians 4:15). Another way to think about this is that truth must be spoken in a context of grace and safety.

Sometimes in the church we can get this wrong. We know that truth is important, so we hammer people with the truth about their behavior, hoping this will get them to change and grow. But if the context of grace and safety isn't in place, the truth isn't likely to land, and it may damage the relationship beyond repair. A better option is to focus on grace and safety first, until the relationship is better developed. If you have some truth you would like to share, hold off at first. Keep the truth in your back pocket until the grace and safety have time to develop. Then you can begin to incorporate truth and feedback into your relationship.

As Joseph and Sallie grew more comfortable in their group, they were more open to receiving truth about themselves and their situation. For example, the members encouraged the couple to explore in more detail their fear of judgment from others regarding Jerrod and his behavior, as well as their foster care journey. Joseph and Sallie realized that they placed a lot of weight and importance on other people (family, friends, and even strangers) thinking they were "good parents." They yearned for the approval of others. This fear of judgment and disapproval held them back from fully loving and accepting Jerrod. Because the context of grace and safety were in place in the group, Joseph and Sallie were more open to explore this area of growth and be honest about it.

Back to Grace

Although I have been talking about grace and safety leading to vulnerability and truth, increased levels of vulnerability and truth can also lead to deeper experiences of grace and safety over time (J. P. Hook et al., 2017). The relationship is reciprocal. Here's why: if I only share a little bit of myself with you, if I'm only a little vulnerable, you might accept me and offer me grace, but you're only accepting a small piece of me because I'm hiding the other parts. I might think to myself, *Okay, she's accepting me, but what would happen if she knew [fill in the blank]? She might reject me and then I might be in real trouble.* This is why if you only have a little bit of vulnerability, you likely will only experience a little bit of grace and support. But if you take the risk and have full vulnerability, you give yourself the opportunity to experience a large amount of grace and support.

When it comes down to it, this is what emotional support is all about. We create a context of grace and safety in relationship with others where we can be vulnerable and reveal our true selves. We also trust each other and give each other permission to help us see the truth about ourselves and our situation. When we share vulnerably with each other, we give each other grace when we need it. We stick together. We help one another when we stumble and fall. We carry each other's burdens (Galatians 6:2).

Me Too

In emotionally supportive relationships we say, "Me too." We understand that we share similar experiences and have similar journeys. Even if we don't have exactly the same experience, we understand that we all struggle and need grace. This is another way that emotionally supportive relationships embody the gospel. We all have areas of brokenness in our own lives and families. We're in this together, and we need the help of God, as well as others in our community, to not only survive but thrive.

I remember two grandparents who had become kinship caregivers for their three grandchildren, including one who had severe autism. The grandparents received a phone call one evening from a caseworker who informed them that their son and his girlfriend were homeless and addicted to drugs, and it was not safe for the children to be in their care. Within a few hours, the grandchildren were dropped off at their home, and they were neck deep in paperwork and training to get their foster care license. They shared how hard this journey was for them. They loved their grandchildren deeply, and there was no question about placing the children with them. But they didn't sign up for foster care in the same way that other families discern, pray about, and choose it. It took an emotional toll on them. Their son and his girlfriend would call them and demand to see the children, but the state would not allow visits unless they were supervised by the caseworker at the office, and they were only allowed to happen once per week for one hour. Holding that boundary was really stressful for the grandparents' relationship with their son and grandchildren. Additionally, they were in their late fifties and parenting high-needs young children. They felt tired. They were disappointed and angry at their son for making poor life choices. They were heartbroken when their grandkids would ask why their parents wouldn't get sober so that they could be a family again. So many feelings are wrapped up in being a kinship caregiver.

Two things helped them through all these ups and downs: their faith in God and their support network. Even though the specifics of their journey as kinship caregivers looked different, the underlying need for grace, love, and support were the same. When others could hear their struggle and say, "Me too," even without sharing the exact same experience, the kinship caregivers felt a sense of peace amid their struggle. They knew they could get up and do what God called them to do, because they weren't in this journey alone.

The support group was an absolute lifeline for Joseph and Sallie. They finally had a place where they could share their struggles honestly and receive grace rather than judgment or criticism. One particular turning point for them was when Joseph admitted in group that sometimes he regretted taking Jerrod in, and he felt like he was failing to lead his family as God wanted him to. As he shared, he started to tear up and cry. To his surprise, some of the other parents in his group said, "Me too." They had dealt with those feelings as well. Joseph wasn't crazy. He did love Jerrod deeply and was just going through a difficult time. The other families in his group had his back and would help him get through it. They were on this journey together.

How to Get the Help You Need?

We've spoken about the characteristics of emotional support, but how do you seek out emotionally supportive relationships for you and your family? Keep a few key points in mind as you work to develop emotional support in your life.

Identify the Need

If you don't have a clear sense of where your family is and what your needs are, you can't take well-informed, concrete steps to meet those needs. A paper from Josh's graduate school adviser discussed the importance of assessment (Worthington et al., 1995). In studying couples, he had looked at the effects of having the couple do a detailed assessment and therapist feedback session. Couples completed questionnaires and discussed a topic in which they disagreed, and then met with a therapist who discussed the couple's strengths and weaknesses. Where was the couple right now? What key needs should be addressed moving forward? Couples' marriages improved just from the assessment and feedback session. Getting clarity on your needs has power.

Start identifying your needs by thinking about what your life would look like if all your family's emotional support needs were met. In other words, imagine you woke up tomorrow to a miracle. Something magical happened during the night, and a "good enough" level of emotional support is now in place. What would that look like? Who would be involved in the life of you and your kids? How much time (daily, weekly, monthly) would you be spending engaged in supportive relationships?

This *miracle question*, as it is called in solution-focused therapy (de Shazer et al., 2007), is helpful because it can give you a clear sense of your needs. Once you get a sense of that, you can take stock in your present level of emotional support. Who is providing you with emotional support? Who is doing so in your kids' lives? How does your life now and the miracle scenario line up? Is there a big gap between them? That gap represents your needs. Don't feel bad if it's big. This is just a starting place. You need an honest picture of where you are and where you need to go.

A few things came up for Joseph and Sallie when they thought about their emotional support needs. One big realization was that they needed to be in relationship with other families involved in fostering. When they became foster parents, most of their friends expressed happiness and support for them without comprehending the complexities of parenting a child with a difficult upbringing. Sallie and Joseph needed to be in relationship with other parents who could say, "Me too." This was true of their children as well, both their daughters and Jerrod. Their children needed to be with other peers who could say, "Me too, I understand what you're going through." It was also important to surround Jerrod with support and community from his cultural background. The couple also realized that they needed to work on finding families who would be welcoming and receptive to their new family, even with its unique challenges. Some of their friends were a bit uptight about their own children and had a hard time with Jerrod's occasional tendencies to roughhouse. Joseph and Sallie needed to locate families who were a bit more gracious toward Jerrod and willing to learn about trauma and welcome him into friendship with their kids.

Take the Initiative

When my husband, Josh, first went to college, he thought that relationships and community would just happen. Growing up, he had always had a good group of friends and community through school and church, and he figured the same thing would be the case at college. But when he arrived, he found that relationships just didn't happen. After a while, he felt lonely and frustrated with his social situation. In the summer after freshman year, he realized that part of his problem was a lack of initiative. He expected that other people would reach out to him, but he wasn't doing any work in the other direction. He came up with a new plan for sophomore year. He would take the initiative. He went around to everyone on his new floor and introduced himself. Before he went down to the dining hall, he walked around and asked if anyone wanted to join him. He became involved in a campus organization. Then the emotionally supportive friendships began to develop, and his second year was a lot more rewarding and fun.

The responsibility is yours to seek out the emotional support you need. You can't sit back and wait for other people to recognize your needs and meet them. Reach out. Introduce yourself. Meet new people. Ask people to get a meal. In your existing relationships, ask for what you need. Maybe you need to prioritize a date night with your spouse. Can you ask for child care support? Check to see if people are interested and open to going deeper. Be intentional in your relationships and see what happens.

I know taking this step can be hard. I once sat with a family who was deep in the trenches and seeking additional support. We discussed the possibility of respite support one time a month from a consistent family. We wanted the respite support to be focused on building a relationship with them and the other family and not just a one-and-done experience. The goal was that the parents could recharge with a steady night out to look forward to and have a better emotional baseline as a result to continue loving their children well. The parents admitted that having respite support would be helpful, but they expressed feeling embarrassed about needing this kind of support and felt apprehensive about pursuing it. Seeking support was entangled with feelings of insecurity for them—that somehow they failed as parents because they needed someone to step in and help them out. This could not be further from the truth.

Parenting well means recognizing your needs and asking for support so that you can continue giving your best to your children. It does not mean driving a car on an empty gas tank and hoping that the tank magically fills up. It means pulling over and putting gas in your tank so that you can keep driving.

This was a tough suggestion for Joseph and Sallie to incorporate. Joseph was naturally introverted, and engaging in a lot of small talk to meet new people didn't come naturally to him. Meeting new people was easier for Sallie, but she would sometimes get frustrated, feeling like she was doing a lot of work to try and develop relationships that wasn't always reciprocated. Over time, however, the reality that they needed more emotional support became paramount, and they began to be bolder in reaching out to meet new people and find couples and families to connect with. Even Joseph made it a goal to meet one new person at church every Sunday, and he was able to do this even though it was uncomfortable for him.

Be Reciprocal

In order to be sustainable over time, relationships need to be reciprocal. Both parties need to have their needs met. Some level of give-and-take must be present. Be cautious about entering into relationships that are too one-sided. If you want a friend to ask you how you are doing and listen to your pain, make sure you are also spending time doing the same. Make sure the relationship is a two-way street.

Reciprocal relationships can be challenging for adoptive and foster families. Sometimes your level of need can be so high that having any extra energy to help meet the needs of others can be a stretch. And the reality is that you may go through difficult seasons where you need more help and support than average. If you are in one of those seasons now, keep the following suggestions in mind. First, have multiple sources of support. Don't rely on just one or two families. Develop a large team of folks who can support you through your tough time. Second, if your needs for emotional support are very high, consider professional counseling. In this relationship, you are paying the counselor, so the relationship by definition does not require give-and-take. The conversation is completely focused on you and your needs. Don't hesitate to make this part of your routine if you need it.

Sallie and Joseph made it a priority to be reciprocal in their relationships. For example, they would switch off with couples in having each other over or babysitting the kids on weekends. Sometimes they would get exhausted, especially when Jerrod was really struggling, so there were periods when they had to lean on their friends more and couldn't always reciprocate in an equal way. However, they had a large enough support system so that their friends didn't feel taken advantage of or overwhelmed. In some cases, their friends actually saw it as a privilege to serve Joseph and Sallie's family, because it was a way that they could help serve vulnerable children, even though they weren't personally involved in adoption or foster care.

Recognize That Relationships Take Time and Effort

Don't expect a close relationship to develop quickly. Opening up and getting to know someone is a process that you can't rush. Commit to nourishing this relationship over weeks, months, and years. Developing emotionally supportive relationships also takes effort because consistently being in relationship with someone, spending time with them, and working through life's ups and downs is hard work—and it's worth the effort. Apply consistent effort over time, and you will one day reflect in amazement at the level of depth and intimacy that has developed in your closest relationships.

This point was certainly true for Joseph and Sallie. Once they recognized that they needed more emotional support and started taking a greater initiative, relationships took time to develop. Sometimes they would meet a family and feel hopeful that they could become close friends, but the relationship would peter out over the next few months, which was disappointing for Joseph, Sallie, and their kids. But over time, Joseph and Sallie continued to connect with other families, and relationships began to develop and deepen. For example, they met another couple at church who was also fostering, and this couple ended up being their best "couple friends." After a few years of reaching out, they had a great support system in place, with several individuals and families willing to help in times of need.

OPTIONS FOR SUPPORT

Now that you have a sense of how you might reach out and find emotional support, what kinds of emotionally supportive relationships are possible for adoptive and foster families? Before getting into the specific kinds of support that many families find helpful, let's keep two principles in mind.

Principle #1: Develop Supportive Relationships with People inside and outside the Journey

Throughout this chapter I have focused on the idea of "me too." Relationships with other families who are working through similar problems and issues are important—families who really get the unique aspects of adoption and foster care in a deep way. These kinds of relationships are essential so that you as well as your kids know that you are not crazy and you are not alone.

Emotionally supportive relationships with people outside adoption and fostering are also important. One reason is that adoptive and foster families are often busy themselves. They might be overwhelmed in getting their own needs met, as you are. Also, although not all Christians are called to personally adopt or foster, all Christians are called to help and support vulnerable children.

Principle #2: Develop Supportive Relationships for You and Your Kids

Some parents focus on themselves but fail to recognize that kids through adoption or foster care can have a difficult time fitting in and developing connections too. Children, including biological children, need relationships and support during this journey. Some families focus on the kids but fail to recognize that parents need supportive relationships with other adults as well. As you move forward in developing a support team, keep the needs of both generations in mind.

One of the best resources, now popping up all over the United States each summer, are family camps that foster and adoptive parents and their children attend together. There are age-appropriate groups for the children and training times for the parents. While these opportunities are now isolated mostly to the summer months, this important movement is beginning to take shape all year long, mostly via support groups. Take advantage of this opportunity if it's available near you.

Types of Emotionally Supportive Relationships

What types of emotionally supportive relationships are out there? Here we discuss five different types: one-on-one relationships, couples and families, support groups, online support communities, and professional help.

One-on-One Relationships

One-on-one relationships refer to time spent regularly with one other person. For example, Joseph developed a friendship with Greg, an associate pastor at his church. They would grab breakfast one Saturday morning per month and talk about how they were doing. One-on-one relationships are helpful because they provide the time and space to dig in and share with one another in a deep, intimate way. You have the privacy to be honest and devote the time needed to develop a strong bond.

Couples and Families

Through their support group, Joseph and Sallie met fellow foster parents Dave and Candice. When their schedules worked out, they would trade off and have each other over for dinner and their kids would have a play date. Dave and Candice had a foster son around Jerrod's age, so the kids developed a friendship as well. The adults and kids had time to laugh and have fun together.

Getting together with other couples and families is important. Your kids especially get a chance to build relationships with other kids who are adopted or are in foster care, which can help them feel more connected and accepted—which is huge. For many of our children, being adopted or fostered becomes a fundamental part of their identity. I remember sitting in counseling with one little girl and asking her, "What are five things you'd like people to know about you?" Her first response was, "I'm fostered." She could have given any response: I like ponies, my favorite color is purple, I take ballet lessons, my best friend is Ashley. Her answer indicates that children also need to hear and be able to say, "Me too. I'm fostered as well. I know your journey."

This same principle applies for any biological children in your care. Sometimes we can be so focused on supporting the needs and activities of our children through adoption or foster care that we overlook those of our biological children. I remember a foster mother who echoed this sentiment. As a family, they were fostering two boys and had two biological daughters. At one point she realized that they had been so intentional about supporting the boys and making sure they had relationships where they could process their experiences (such as with therapists and mentors), but the same was not true for her biological daughters, even though their need for support was equally as important.

Support Groups

Throughout this chapter we've learned about Joseph and Sallie's participation in their faith-based support group made up of adoptive and foster families. The group met in a host family's home, and the group itself had multiple components. The group began with members socializing and sharing a meal. All the children connected with one another in a different area of the home with trauma-trained child care workers. After the meal, the group opened with a check-in, where each group member shared for one minute about what they were feeling (sad, angry, scared, happy, excited, tender) and gave a brief context for their feeling. Following the check-in, the group leader led the group through a brief devotional, which kicked off a time of sharing and support.

This support group was based on the principles of emotionally supportive relationships discussed earlier (J. P. Hook et al., 2017). First and foremost, the group was a place where group members could receive grace. From the time they started attending the group, Joseph and Sallie were loved and supported right where they were at—without fear of judgment. The group was also safe. The leader set out ground rules for group participation (e.g., confidentiality, no judgments or criticism, consistent attendance to foster deeper relationships), and she instructed members to adhere to the guidelines. The group leader also encouraged vulnerability, where group members could share as much about themselves or their stories as they felt safe sharing. Finally, the group was a place where truth was shared in love, and discipleship occurred. The group wasn't a gripefest; instead, it was a place for adoptive and foster parents who loved their kids to heal, learn, and grow.

Online Support Communities

Although small groups are invaluable—and one of my dreams is to see small groups available everywhere for every family who wants to be a part of one—the reality is that finding a support group or community of people who are doing the hard work of adoption and foster care is not always easy. You might be one of the only families locally involved in adoption or foster care, or you might be involved in a church community that doesn't have a ministry to support vulnerable children and their families in a real, tangible way. If that's the case, you can still receive the emotional support of a group through an online community. For example, Mike and Kristin Berry have developed an online community called Oasis, which offers access to face-to-face support and mentoring, monthly video resources, educational content, and community connection. Bottom line: don't give up if you look around and realize that your needs for emotional support aren't being met in your area. There's still a way to get support from others, although finding the avenue that works best for your family might take a bit of work.

Professional Help

By *professional help*, I mean a licensed counselor, psychologist, or psychiatrist who can help meet your needs for emotional support. Licensed counselors and psychologists provide talk therapy. Psychologists also provide mental health assessments. While some psychiatrists offer talk therapy, most prescribe psychotropic medication. Even the best support team sometimes is no match for consultation with or treatment from a professional because of the services professionals provide and the specific ways they can offer assistance.

Another reason for seeking professional help is if you have a situation with your child that seems overwhelming or is getting out of control. As I talked about in the chapter on stress, children impacted by adoption or foster care often have a history of trauma. Difficult upbringings can lead to a host of attachment, emotional, and behavioral problems that might leave you feeling in over your head, and that's okay. Don't feel shame about getting extra help for you or your child if you need it. Surrounding your family with all the help and support you can find, including the support of a professional, is actually wise and courageous.

When looking for a counselor or therapist, please follow these suggestions. Find a licensed mental health professional. Counselors, social workers, and psychologists go through years of education and supervised clinical training. You want someone with experience who knows what she is doing. Second, find a professional with expertise in the area in which you or your child are struggling. If you want help improving family relationships, seek out someone with expertise in family therapy. If you want help with your marriage, go to a person with expertise in couples counseling. If you want help for your child, find a counselor who has experience with kids who have a history of trauma. Finally, interview a few counselors before making a decision. A significant part of successful counseling is the therapeutic relationship between the counselor and the client(s) (Horvath & Greenberg, 1994). Make sure you choose a counselor with whom you feel like you can connect and develop a good rapport. Counselors have a variety of interpersonal styles. Some are more directive, whereas others let the client take the lead. Some are more formal; others are more laid-back. It's an important relationship, so don't rush into it and don't settle.

Also, parents whose kids are having serious difficulties should consult with a psychiatrist to consider psychotropic medication. Some Christians feel uneasy or even resistant to psychotropic medication, but for certain children it can be invaluable. I consulted with a family whose foster child exhibited dysregulated behavior, and I thought the child might benefit from psychotropic medication, or at least a consult. The family disagreed, believing that the child was "just sinning," or "it was the devil in him that was causing him to act that way." We do a complete disservice to ourselves and to our children when we think mental health problems are entirely within our control. Mental health issues are real, to be treated just like physical symptoms or illnesses. You would never suggest that a child suffering from asthma should just push through those asthma attacks. You'd get him the help he needs: an inhaler, so he can function better. Trauma affects the brain, which is directly linked to our emotions and behaviors. Neurotransmitters are firing on a regular basis, and if those are out of whack, psychotropic medication can help get us back on track. That goes for parents as well. No shame comes in taking necessary physician-prescribed medication for its intended purpose.

Psychotropic medication can also improve a child's emotional baseline so that they can make progress in counseling. Posttraumatic stress disorder, anxiety disorders, depressive disorders, and attention-deficit/hyperactivity disorder, among others, all impact our brain chemistry. I remember getting a counseling referral for a seven-year-old boy whose licensing agency was considering residential treatment because his aggression was so severe that they could not find any foster parents willing to take him. He initially struggled to make any progress in counseling because he was so dysregulated. We had to get his brain what it needed to manage his emotions and lessen the impact of his triggers. Once he saw a psychiatrist and got on the correct medication, he calmed down and made significant progress in therapy. It was as if he no longer had to push a boulder up the hill, but just climb. His aggressive behaviors disappeared almost entirely, and we were able to see his true, precious self.

Joseph and Sallie did eventually seek out the help of a licensed clinical psychologist to help their family cope with some of their adjustments following Jerrod's placement into their home. The counselor, Dr. Stuart, was an experienced family therapist who had been involved in clinical practice for over twenty-five years. She also had specific training counseling adolescents and children with trauma. At first, Joseph and Sallie attended sessions as a couple, to talk with Dr. Stuart about their goals and what they wanted out of counseling. Then they began to see Dr. Stuart as a family. It took some time, but Joseph and Sallie noticed that the family dynamics, especially between Jerrod and their daughters, slowly began to improve. For example, as a result of therapy, Jerrod, Grace, and Lilly were better able to use their words to describe what they were feeling, rather than acting out by hitting or shoving. Joseph and Sallie also felt relieved that they had a professional whom they could go to for help and advice. At one point in treatment, Dr. Stuart also referred Sallie to a psychiatrist for a medication consult. Sallie recognized that she no longer felt like herself and was battling with feelings of anxiety and depression. She was initially skeptical of medication, but once she started the psychotropic medication and began to feel better, she said it was the best decision she ever made.

Exercise: Finding the Emotional Support You Need

Think about your relationships with other individuals, couples, and families. To what extent are these relationships providing you with a sense of grace for where you are in your adoption or foster care journey?

_____

_____

_____

_____

_____

How safe are these relationships? How often do you experience judgment, criticism, or advice giving? Do you experience anything else that makes the relationship feel less safe?

_____

_____

_____

_____

_____

How vulnerable can you be in these relationships? To what extent can you take off your masks and let people see who you really are? How vulnerable are they with you?

_____

_____

_____

_____

_____

_____

How much truth can you tell them? Are you open to hearing truth and feedback from them about you and your life? Are these relationships causing you to heal, grow, and change for the better, or do they feel stagnant?

_____

_____

_____

_____

_____

_____

Think about the different types of emotional support: one-on-one relationships, couples and families, support groups, online support communities, and professional help. Which of these sources of support have you tapped into? Which might be a next step for you and your family?

_____

_____

_____

_____

_____

_____

After reading this chapter, what one next step would you like to take in order to improve the level of emotional support for you and your family?

_____

_____

_____

_____

_____

_____

CHAPTER 5

The Sunlight
Informational Support

An investment in knowledge always pays the best interest.

—BENJAMIN FRANKLIN

IN THE PREVIOUS chapter, we talked about the first key aspect of support: emotional support, or the good soil. In this chapter, we focus on the second key aspect of support: informational support. Informational support gets at the knowledge and wisdom necessary to parent children from hard places and can be thought of as the sunlight that illuminates your path and stimulates growth.

Light is often used as a metaphor in the Bible to represent God and God's wisdom. For example, the Psalmist describes God's word as a lamp for his feet and a light for his path (Psalm 119:105). Jesus describes himself as the light of the world and promises that who-ever follows him will never walk in darkness, but will have the light of life (John 8:12). God is described as light, and we are likewise called to walk in the light: "God is light; in him there is no darkness at all. If we claim to have fellowship with him and yet walk in the darkness, we lie and do not live in the truth. But if we walk in the light, as he is in the light, we have fellowship with one another, and the blood of Jesus, his Son, purifies us from all sin" (1 John 1:5–7).

Parenting children can be complex, especially when children have trauma histories. Typically, we parent our children based on how we were parented (Firestone, 2012). We default to what we know and how we were raised, and this parenting strategy usually works for children raised in fairly healthy, well-adjusted homes. But some of us grew up with parents who had significant limitations and problems, and raising our kids in the same way our parents raised us may not be beneficial.

This problem is exacerbated especially when you are raising children from hard places. When children have experienced trauma, traditional parenting practices, such as consequences and time-outs, can backfire (Purvis, Cross, & Sunshine, 2007). When I was growing up, my parents loved to use "1, 2, 3 magic." When they were getting close to the count of three, I knew I had to respond with compliance. However, as we learned in chapter 2, kids from hard places with trauma histories are often operating on emotion alone; sometimes their emotion regulation and reasoning capacities are even switched off. They may have a difficult time developing a secure attachment. As a result, you may need to use unique or different parenting strategies to help your child. This is why trauma-informed parenting is so important. Parents who simply do what they know or observed from their parents aren't giving themselves or their children the best chances to thrive. It's as if families are wandering in the darkness, not knowing where to find the light. This chapter is designed to help adoptive and foster families find that informational light. First, I go over some key foundational principles that can help when parenting a child from a hard place. Then I discuss a variety of ways that parents can find informational support and how to put together a plan to get the informational support you need.

DOUGLAS AND RACHAEL

Douglas and Rachael were in their mid-thirties when they met at the singles ministry at their church. They dated, fell in love, and married within a year. Both of them wanted children, so they started trying to get pregnant right away. When they didn't get pregnant within the first year of marriage, they sought the help of a fertility doctor. They tried a variety of options, including acupuncture and hormone treatments. However, after some time, the doctor determined that in vitro fertilization (IVF) was the only other option in order for them to have a chance of getting pregnant. Douglas and Rachael seriously considered IVF, but ended up deciding that they didn't feel comfortable moving forward in that direction. Instead, they began to seek discernment and pray about whether adoption might be the route they should take to build their family.

After about a year of thinking, discussing, and praying, Rachael and Douglas decided that they wanted to pursue domestic adoption and began the process of working with an adoption agency, preparing their home for the home study, and putting together the information to give potential biological mothers who were making an adoption plan for their child. There were tough decisions to make. Did they want an infant, or were they open to adopting an older child? Did they have preferences about the gender or race or ethnicity of the child? How restrictive or open did they want to be about various factors about the biological mother (e.g., substance-exposed)?

They ended up adopting a six-month-old baby girl named Brelynn. Brelynn's mother was having trouble caring for five other biological children and decided to make an adoption plan for Brelynn. There were some complications around the adoption: Brelynn's mom had been evicted during the pregnancy and had spent some time in a shelter before being placed in low-income housing. She had also struggled with the final decision about the adoption, changing her mind a few times (once even after the baby was born). So, there was quite a bit of stress leading up to the time that Douglas and Rachael took Brelynn in to be with them. They were nervous about the grace period where Brelynn's mom could change her mind. But no call came, and the adoption was finalized.

The early years of Brelynn's life were both joyous and difficult. Douglas and especially Rachael loved being parents. They enjoyed getting to know Brelynn, playing with her, and watching her learn new things. When Brelynn first learned to say "Mama," Rachael's heart felt so full, as if it could burst. They also enjoyed their new roles as mother and father. Most of their friends were around the same age as they were and had families of their own. Douglas and Rachael had felt a bit out of step because they had married later and didn't have any kids. Now they felt like they fit in more with their friends and could connect with them in a new and deeper way.

But parenting was also a difficult adjustment for the couple. Brelynn was a more difficult child than average, and Douglas and Rachael weren't really expecting it. Because Brelynn didn't have any visible developmental problems or substance exposure, Douglas and Rachael anticipated her developing like a normal baby. They were caught off guard when Brelynn had some developmental problems. Specifically, she began to miss some of her developmental milestones, and both Rachael and Douglas tried to soothe her, often unsuccessfully. Brelynn also had a hard time sleeping through the night, which made Douglas and Rachael's level of stress and exhaustion even worse.

Douglas and Rachael both grew up in solid homes with available parents. They knew that parenting would be an adjustment and a learning experience, but they soon realized that they were unprepared for parenting Brelynn. The normal kinds of parenting techniques that their parents or other families tried (e.g., time-outs, taking away allowance and privileges) didn't seem to work with Brelynn. As she grew older, nothing seemed to motivate good behavior in her. She would scream and lose her temper when Douglas and Rachael threatened to take away privileges, but this didn't really translate into improved behavior at home or at school.

The couple would go to their parents or friends for advice, and they received a lot of it from their community on what to do or try. But nothing really ever seemed to work. At the advice of one of their friends, they even set up an elaborate system of points and rewards around the house, where Brelynn would have to earn every single privilege by performing various tasks or participating in family life. The system took a few weeks for Douglas and Rachael to set up and implement, and it didn't change a thing. Brelynn just shrugged her shoulders, said she wasn't going to do it, and went to her room.

Maybe you can relate to Douglas and Rachael's experience. If you are doing the difficult work of parenting a child from a hard place, you probably have come to a similar point in your life. The normal parenting strategies don't seem to be working. You might get a lot of advice from family and friends, but the advice doesn't seem to work either. You feel stuck. You're putting in a lot of effort but not seeing any improvement. You feel like there has to be a more effective way forward, you just don't know what it is.

PARENTING KIDS FROM HARD PLACES

The good news is that information is available out there that can help you parent a struggling child. You don't have to go at it alone. Some concepts and practices can help put you in the best possible position to parent your child. Does that mean all your child's problems will be fixed? No, because life still happens, and parenting is not easy. But you are more likely to be an effective parent if you have the information you need.

When I was working as a therapist with kids in foster care, I was struggling myself. I had been trained as a clinician, but our program didn't have a specific trauma focus for working with kids. The traditional methods weren't helping, and I knew that I needed something more. I sought out additional training and began studying Trust-Based Relational Intervention (TBRI; Purvis et al., 2013). I eventually took additional supervised training in this approach and became a TBRI educator. TBRI was an absolute game-changer in my work with foster children, informing many of my key principles for thinking about supporting vulnerable children. (I include information on TBRI resources in the appendices.) In addition to increasing my knowledge, the process of seeking out additional training and knowledge itself was helpful for me as a professional. I was taking the initiative to learn more and empower my work. I always want to be learning and growing in my work, and parents should have this same attitude.

Before I talk about some helpful information for parenting children from hard places, I want to be clear: your success as a parent is not dependent on your child's outcome. I know that, for some of you, parenting a child who has been abused, neglected, and abandoned has wreaked havoc on your life and your family's life. You may be parenting older children or children with significant challenges and nothing seems to help. I've worked with families that have had to implement safety plans in their home and have the local police phone number on speed dial. Parenting children who have experienced trauma is complex, and no one-size-fits-all approach or magic wand leads our children to healing. You become trauma-aware, implement therapeutic parenting strategies, understand what your child is experiencing physiologically in their bodies when they become triggered, and then do the best you can.

But whether this new information leads to positive outcomes for your child or not should never call into question your success as a parent. I remember a mom who shared that when her adolescent son would become triggered, there was a ripple effect on the other children. They would inevitably become triggered, and each had different ways of responding. One child would become aggressive and punch holes in the wall, and another child would run out of the house. I remember her wrestling with how to meet each child's needs when they respond so differently. *How do I connect with each child?* Learning about your child and what works for that particular one requires more than a cookie-cutter approach. Give yourself space to try a variety of things. You're not failing. You're learning about your children, what they need, and what can bring about certain responses or reactions. God is creative enough to give multiple people resources and tools that are effective for helping your child.

TWO KEY ISSUES IN RAISING CHILDREN IMPACTED BY ADOPTION AND FOSTER CARE

In what follows, I share two key issues you need to understand when you are raising children through adoption or foster care—or, really, if you are in community with them in any fashion: attachment and trauma.

Attachment

Attachment refers to a deep, enduring emotional bond that connects two people across time and situations (Ainsworth, 1973; Bowlby, 1969). For most people, the primary attachment bond occurs between a baby and one's primary caregivers, especially the mother. Attachment theory originated with the work of John Bowlby, who worked as a child psychiatrist in London. Coming out of his work with emotionally disturbed children, Bowlby began to outline the important role of the emotional bond between mother and child, and the impact that this bond has on a child's social, emotional, and cognitive development (Bowlby, 1958).

Mary Ainsworth was a developmental psychologist who built on John Bowlby's theorizing and work on attachment. Specifically, Ainsworth found that infants displayed different types of attachment styles, and the styles related to early experiences with their primary caregivers (Ainsworth et al., 1978). She found three main types of attachment. The first was *secure attachment*. Babies who were securely attached were comfortable with closeness and intimacy, and also were comfortable exploring their environment. The second was *anxious attachment*. Anxiously attached babies had a hard time when they were separated from their primary caregiver, and they also had a tough time settling down once they were reunited with their primary caregiver. The third was *avoidant attachment*. Babies who were avoidantly attached didn't seem to worry too much when they were separated from their primary caregiver and had trouble connecting with them.

Some evidence exists that early parenting styles are related to a baby's attachment style (Ainsworth et al., 1978). If parents do a good enough job of meeting a baby's needs and comforting the baby when necessary, the baby is likely to develop a secure attachment. The baby begins to trust the primary caregiver to meet her needs. The baby has a need, the baby cries, and the caregiver comes to meet the need. Rinse, wash, repeat. However, if parents or caregivers fail to meet a baby's early needs, the child might develop an avoidant attachment style. If the parents are inconsistent in meeting a baby's early needs, an anxious attachment style might result.

Many children involved in adoption and foster care have challenges developing a secure attachment, and it's easy to understand why. Children in foster care often have experienced early abuse or neglect. Adopted children likely struggled to have early needs met for love and affection. Some developmental psychologists theorize that the attachment relationship begins before the child is even born, as the infant stays in tune with the mother's heartbeat, voice, and other biological markers (Brhel, 2009). The fetus is capable of feeling, and this emotional attachment with the mother is affected by the neurohormonal dialogue between them, meaning that if Mom is experiencing high stress, the anxiety is not only pulsing through her body but through the unborn baby as well. Thus, even if you adopted your child at birth, there still may be difficulties in developing a secure attachment relationship.

Mike and Kristin Berry adopted their child at birth. They held her in their arms just minutes after she entered the world. Mike fed the newborn her first bottle and Kristin changed her first diaper. Her birth mother took very good care of herself throughout the pregnancy, eating healthy, taking prenatal vitamins. Most people would look at this situation and conclude, "No trauma. Instant bonding. Everything is normal." For the most part, it was. But think about this: their daughter spent the first nine months of her life in another human being's womb, listening to her voice, feeling her warmth, and experiencing (to a degree) what she experienced. Then, she was separated from that. This produces a level of trauma. Today, she is a normal, happy, healthy teenager who is completely bonded to them. But the trauma of separation lingered until a few years ago.

Secure Base

What do these struggles with attachment mean for adoptive and foster parents now? One of the most helpful models I have seen for helping a child's attachment is the Circle of Security (Hoffman et al., 2017). In the Circle of Security, the role of parenting on attachment is thought to have two main functions. First, the parents function as a *secure base*. Remember when you played tag as a kid? There was a home base where you could go and be safe from getting tagged. The idea of a secure base is similar. As parents, you provide a secure place for a child to call home and get their needs met. The secure base isn't going anywhere. Your children can rely on it.

Having a secure base allows children to venture out into the world and explore. Just like the game of tag, you can't stay at home base forever. You have to get out there and play the game. In a similar way, children need to venture out, go to school, make friends, and get involved with activities. Having a secure base allows children to feel confident about living their lives.

Safe Haven

The world out there is sometimes scary and can feel dangerous. We feel that as adults, so imagine how foster or adopted children feel from their starting points. A scraped knee is a normal part of growing up, but events like these can still be difficult for a kid from a hard place. When tough things happen, these kids need somewhere to go to be comforted and get their needs met. This is the second function of parenting on attachment, the *safe haven*. When children have trouble getting grounded out in the world, they need to know they can come back for protection and comfort. They need to know they can rely on their parents.

This cycle of interactions can build secure attachment in children over time. As parents, you provide a secure base through meeting your child's needs consistently. As children start to feel this secure base, they can then venture out and begin to interact with the world.

Helping Kids Build Secure Attachment

Parents can do three key things to help build a secure attachment with their children. First, *work on your own attachment security*. None of us had perfect parents. If you're anything like me, your parents probably had strengths and limitations, positive qualities and faults. I grew up on a farm in rural Canada. My parents were always there for me physically but sometimes struggled to know about my emotional needs. Did your parents provide a secure base? Were they consistent in meeting your physical and emotional needs? What about when you explored your environment and something went wrong, and maybe you got hurt? Did they comfort you or tell you to get over it?

One of the strongest predictors of the attachment style your child will develop is the attachment style you had with your own parents (Firestone, 2015). That is, you are likely to pass your attachment style on to your children. If you had an insecure attachment with your parents, you may continue this style of relating as an adult and parent (McConnell & Moss, 2011). If you have an insecure attachment style as an adult, your child may not develop a secure attachment to you. Sometimes we tend to blame attachment problems on the child impacted by trauma, but attachment is a two-way street. It's important for parents to do their own work. It's difficult to bring a child to a place we haven't been ourselves. How comfortable are you with physical touch, talking about feelings, or giving and receiving when people (including you) are hurting? You can talk these issues over with a counselor. Attachment styles are not set in stone, and you can change them with therapeutic work.

Second, *consistently meet your children's physical and emotional needs.* We all have certain basic needs (Maslow, 1943): biological, like food and water; safety, such as living in a secure and danger-free home; and love and belonging—physical and verbal.

Children through adoption or foster care may not have had basic needs met, and moreover, adoptive and foster families are often working with incomplete information about their children's histories. For example, Jessica was neglected and didn't get enough to eat as a child, and she tended to hoard food. Gary lived in an unsafe environment in his early years and would often act out physically in order to protect himself. Lori, who was abused and neglected as a young child, tried to gain love and affection in inappropriate ways. As parents, first meet your child's basic needs for nourishment and security. That's the foundation for moving on to bigger emotional stakes. Sometimes kids just need to know that food and the same bed will be there no matter what.

Third, *help soothe and co-regulate the child when she is hurting.* Children from hard places are often unable to self-soothe when something goes wrong. An important part of effective early parenting is soothing youngsters when they are distressed. For example, instead of just telling Brelynn to "calm down" (which didn't work), Rachael began to hold Brelynn and slowly rock her, helping to co-regulate Brelynn's emotions. In those situations, a baby begins to learn, *If I am hurting or in pain, I can cry and reach out, and I will get my needs met.* Over time, as the child grows older, she learns how to self-soothe and meet her own needs when things go wrong or are difficult. It is as if they have internalized the primary caregiver.

Children impacted by the loss of their first family may have missed out on this key piece of attachment security. When they were in pain and cried for help, nothing happened. Even worse, they may have been punished or abused for reaching out. They don't trust that their needs for comfort will be met, and they have not been able to self-soothe or comfort themselves when in distress. Again, the key here is consistent *soothing* and co-regulation. If the child cannot self-soothe and self-regulate, the parent can help through calming physical touch and verbal reassurances. Over time, the hope is that the child can learn what's been missed to that point in their development.

From the beginning of the adoption, Brelynn's attachment to Douglas and Rachael was uncertain. Brelynn showed signs of *anxious attachment,* meaning that she would cry and yell when Douglas or Rachael would try to put her down, but she also had a difficult time calming down when Douglas or Rachael attempted to soothe her; both were likely related to her early upbringing. Brelynn's mother experienced a high level of anxiety during pregnancy, and during Brelynn's first months of life, five older siblings consumed her mother's energy and attention. Brelynn would cry for her mother to meet a need, but Brelynn's mother wasn't always physically or emotionally available.

After learning about attachment and the Circle of Security, Douglas and Rachael committed to being consistent in providing a secure base and safe haven for Brelynn. Even though Douglas wasn't exactly comfortable with touch—due partly to his relationship with his own parents, who were on the emotionally cold side—he really tried to work on this part of himself for Brelynn's sake. Douglas and Rachael gave Brelynn hugs and kisses and "I love yous" every day, even when they were mad and didn't feel like it. They also committed to being consistent with trying to soothe and co-regulate Brelynn when she would get upset. Instead of getting into power struggles, they would calmly address Brelynn's behavior and emotion. After a few years, Brelynn finally learned how to calm herself down.

Trauma-Informed Parenting

We've discussed trauma throughout the book, but to recap, trauma refers to a major injury that can have long-lasting effects on an individual. Trauma can be physical (hitting, slapping, beating), emotional (yelling, put-downs, silence), sexual (unwanted sexual advances, rape), or neglectful (failing to meet basic safety and emotional needs). Children who are adopted or involved in the foster system have often experienced trauma of some kind. What are some important points to keep in mind when parenting a child who has trauma in his or her background?

Think Survival, Not Disobedience

Adoptive and foster families should consider reframing their children's behavior as coming from a place of hurt and survival rather than willful disobedience. Children in situations where they are being abused or neglected are doing whatever they can in order to make it. They are in survival mode. If their biological parents neglected them, for example, they may have had to hoard food *because their life depended on it.* Even though they are now in a home with full cupboards, their brain is still in survival mode. When you view your child's behavior in the context of survival rather than disobedience, two positive things happen. First, you are likely to experience higher levels of empathy and compassion for your child.

Second, you are more likely to come up with a creative solution to meet your child's need rather than engaging in another punitive discipline strategy that is unlikely to be effective.

Douglas and Rachael tried hard to rewire their understanding of Brelynn's behavior. This was difficult, especially when Douglas and Rachael were worn out and running low on energy. Douglas would try to remind himself, *She's only doing what she knows*. They would also try to key in on the need behind Brelynn's behavior. For example, they realized that when Brelynn whined and screamed, the need behind her behavior was connection and a desire to know that her needs and voice mattered. Rachael would get in the habit of saying, "Brelynn, I'm here and I'm not going anywhere. What do you need right now?" Viewing Brelynn's behavior in the context of survival helped Douglas and Rachael empathize and have more compassion.

Connection Is the Priority

Because you are trying to rebuild a damaged attachment system, parenting techniques that primarily utilize distance and disconnection can exacerbate the child's fear and trauma response, leading to still more negative outcomes. On the other hand, parenting techniques that emphasize parent-child connection and bonding are likely to result in better outcomes.

I once worked with a foster mother caring for a three-year-old girl who would have prolonged temper tantrums. This mother shared that when her daughter would begin these episodes, the mother would leave the room or ignore her daughter until she calmed down, partly because the screaming was so loud that the mother felt she needed a break. We talked about the girl's history, and I shared about trauma's impact on children. I wondered if this girl needed connection, a secure base, and someone to help her soothe when she was upset. This little girl needed to know that she was seen and loved, even in the mess of her tantrums. I encouraged this foster mom to stay present when the little girl got upset instead of leaving her alone or ignoring her—to continue sitting with her, modeling coping skills and reassuring her. The following week when the foster mother returned, she was flabbergasted. Just sitting next to her foster daughter and reassuring her resulted in huge progress. Instead of having multiple hourlong screaming episodes a day, she had almost none.

Time-outs for children raise another issue, which we've also mentioned. For kids with a history of trauma, time-outs can exacerbate feelings of abandonment and disconnection, which works against what parents want to accomplish. A simple adjustment to the traditional time-out is a *time-in*; when a child misbehaves, stay connected to him. Help him use coping strategies to calm down and show him you are right there with him. Once he is calm, talk about what happened. Instead of sending him to his room or a corner, stay in contact during the time-in. Don't force the child to do something on his own as a punishment, such as clean up a mess by himself, but stay with the child and clean up the mess together to maintain connection.

When Douglas and Rachael learned about prioritizing connection, they worked on changing some of their parenting methods. They no longer sent Brelynn to her room by herself; instead, they used time-ins, sometimes even holding her in their arms as they talked about her behavior and what she could do differently next time. Prioritizing connection helped Brelynn build a foundation of trust, which allowed them to playfully rehearse redos so that she could have a positive experience of rehearsing her behavior in an appropriate way.

Build the Trust Bank

With children who come from hard places, many parents spend a lot of time and energy on discipline or helping control or reduce unwanted behavior, but relatively little time and energy are devoted to more positive interactions, such as positive touch, play, and verbal affirmation. The negative interactions outweighing the positive, however, is understandable. A child's negative behavior can often be highly distressing and require an immediate response.

The problem is that a child's negative behavior can occur frequently, draining the parents' capacity to cope. The parent might be exhausted from the child's problematic behavior as well as life's other demands, so when things are calm, parents might just enjoy the break. Engaging with the child when things are going well doesn't have any particular urgency.

If left unchecked, this pattern can lead to a situation in which the vast majority of parent-child interactions are negative: disciplining, punishing, correcting, and so on. Very few positive interactions take place. With this imbalance, children may be less willing to listen or respond as desired.

Think about interactions with your child as a trust bank. Every time you have a positive interaction with your child, you are making a deposit; every negative interaction is a withdrawal. If you try to make a withdrawal when the account is empty, your check bounces, which in this case means that your child is less likely to respond to your correction in a positive manner. On the other hand, when you have enough money in the bank, the check goes through; that is, your child is more likely to respond to your correction positively when the relationship often includes other positive interactions. Whenever parents tell me that their child consistently responds negatively to discipline and correction, I think about the trust bank.

One of the challenges of parenting a child through adoption or foster care is that you often don't start with the bank accounts at zero. A child with a history of trauma comes to you with a negative balance in the trust bank. Thus, early on, you often have to work extra hard to keep making deposits, even when your child is not responding well to discipline or correction. Remaining positive can be challenging, especially if you are under a high level of stress from other commitments. This is another reason why clearly understanding your limits is so important. You have to be ready to build trust with a child who is initially completely against the idea, and even or especially when you may not feel like it or receive any affirmation in return.

You might think that you need to have one positive interaction for each negative interaction to keep a positive balance in the trust bank. Unfortunately, a one-to-one ratio isn't likely to be enough. As human beings, we are wired to pay more attention to negative events than positive events. This may be related to our evolutionary history and need for survival. Also, quite simply, the bad is stronger than the good (Baumeister et al., 2001). Regarding ratios of types of interactions, in a study of married couples, psychologist John Gottman found that healthy marriages had a ratio of five positive interactions to one negative interaction (Gottman & Silver, 1999). In your interactions with your children, aim for this ratio of five-to-one or higher, daily.

This suggestion was perhaps the most difficult for Douglas and Rachael to follow. Especially for Douglas, he felt maxed out between his work and parenting duties. A fair number of negative interactions took place between Douglas and Brelynn (disciplining, correcting), and he felt overwhelmed about the thought of trying to have five times as many positive interactions as negative ones. He tried to start small. For example, he decided that he would prepare Brelynn breakfast each morning, and they would have a special time together eating oatmeal and reading something from the Bible. He also decided to go out for Dunkin' Donuts with Brelynn every Saturday morning, which also allowed Rachael to get some much-needed rest. As Brelynn grew older, finding things to connect over became easier. For example, Brelynn really liked playing soccer, which Douglas enjoyed also. Douglas decided to volunteer as a coach for Brelynn's park district team, increasing the time they spent together and their positive interactions.

Consider Sensory Processing Challenges

Many children with a trauma history also have sensory processing difficulties (SPD), which can persist even after children have made progress in overcoming their trauma. What are sensory processing difficulties? Our central nervous system receives messages from our senses—auditory (hearing), visual (seeing), tactile (touching), smell, taste, vestibular (balance), and proprioceptive (sense of where your body is in space)—and uses that information to make appropriate decisions related to motor or behavioral responses. However, children with SPD have difficulty processing, organizing, and interpreting the sensory stimuli they receive to function smoothly in everyday life.

For example, take a moment to absorb all the sensory inputs currently around you. Maybe you hear the hum of a heater or air conditioner, the dishwasher running, or cars passing. Your eyes are generally processing a constantly changing visual field. You might smell fresh coffee. If your sensory processing system is working normally, you can filter out most of these inputs and focus on your particular moment or situation. For children with SPD, however, all of their senses are coming in at the same level of intensity, "volume," and children are unable to sort and prioritize them.

SPD often goes undetected in children because many of its symptoms mimic other childhood disorders, such as attention deficit hyperactivity disorder (ADHD) and some learning disabilities. Here are some of the key types of symptoms we see with children who have SPD:

- *Behavioral symptoms.* Withdrawal from being touched, refusal to eat certain foods, hypersensitivity to certain fabrics or tags, dislike of hands being dirty, oversensitivity to odors or sounds, tendency to notice or hear background noises that others cannot, tendency to harm others accidentally during physical play, lack of engagement in creative play.
- *Physical symptoms.* Fatigue; excessive jumping, spinning, and swinging; poor coordination or balance; high pain tolerance; clumsiness; delayed gross and fine motor skills; constant motion.
- *Psychosocial symptoms.* Standing too closely to others, fear of crowds, fear of surprise touch, decreased ability to interact with peers, depression, or anxiety.

SPD has three main subtypes (Kranowitz, 2006). First, children with *sensory modulation disorder* have problems regulating or modulating the intensity and nature of responses to sensory input. Children who are *sensory over-responsive* tend to experience sensory overload. They may find average noises ear-piercing, dislike textured foods, avoid messy textures or other situations, or experience the slightest touch as painful. Children who are *sensory under-responsive* can appear more lethargic, passive, or unaffected by sensory stimulation unless it is very intense. These children may seem unmotivated, be unaware of pain and sickness, have trouble waking up each morning, have difficulty distinguishing between hot and cold, be underestimated when it comes to ability or intelligence, and have difficulty starting tasks. Children who are *sensory seeking* crave sensation. They love spinning, hanging upside down, jumping, or crashing. They love to touch everything and have difficulty understanding the distinction between their space and others'. Sensory seekers are often thought to have ADHD, but a notable difference is that when sensory seekers receive higher levels of sensory input, they actually become more disorganized.

Children with *sensory discrimination disorder* have problems recognizing and interpreting stimuli, assign improper meaning to sensory messages, and have poor detection of differences or similarities in stimuli. Basically, the brain sometimes jumbles or confuses the stimuli. For example, children may have difficulty distinguishing between the words *cat* and *cap*. These children may use too much or too little force or have poor balance, have difficulty distinguishing between similar sounds, or have problems finding an image in a cluttered background. They may not know if they are falling to the side or backward.

Children with *sensory-based motor disorder* have difficulties with balance, fine motor skills, and gross motor skills for familiar, novel, and skilled movements. The two types of sensory-based motor disorders are postural-ocular disorder and dyspraxia (motor planning problem). Children with postural-ocular disorder typically have poor postural control and a hard time maintaining good standing or sitting positions, have difficulty maintaining stability with pushing or pulling, or have improper resistance to objects. Children with dyspraxia have difficulty processing sensory information properly, causing problems with planning and executing functional movement patterns. For example, these children may have difficulty knowing how to put on a new shirt. They may struggle with coordination, specifically with ball games or sports.

If you suspect that a child may have an SPD, you should schedule an appointment with an occupational therapist (OT) for an evaluation. OTs, who work in private practice and school settings, are professionals whose training includes helping children with sensory processing issues. An OT might work with a child who is sensory avoidant by trying to limit sensory exposure or outfitting you with resources to help reduce the child's sensory overload; a child who is sensitive to sound, for example, may need to wear earplugs in loud environments. If you have a child who is sensory seeking, OTs might help create a sensory diet for use in school and home environments to help a child regulate their sensory inputs (e.g., jumping on a mini trampoline or using a weighted blanket). The OT can also provide recommendations related to sensory products that help meet your child's sensory needs. All this can be instrumental in helping your child feel more comfortable, improve their self-regulation skills, and improve the ability to focus.

WHERE CAN I FIND INFORMATIONAL SUPPORT?

Because knowledge about trauma and attachment is so important for adoptive and foster families, having solid sources for quality information is paramount. No summary can cover everything, because each child has a unique set of needs. But in the rest of the chapter, I discuss five sources of information that you might find helpful. Finally, I touch on a situation that is a reality for almost all adoptive and foster families: dealing with limited information.

Books

Even if you don't think of yourself as much of a reader, try to be reading along in one book about trauma-informed parenting at all times. Maybe read for a short time before you go to sleep, or even better, read together with your spouse or support group. Then you can share the information you are learning and discuss implementing it in your lives.

A bunch of books have aided in my own thinking and development in working with children from tough places, and I mention five here.

- *The Connected Child: Bring Hope and Healing to Your Adoptive Family* by Karyn Purvis, David Cross, and Wendy Sunshine (2007) is a comprehensive resource on how to parent children impacted by adoption or foster care, with a particular focus on parenting children who have experienced trauma.

- *Wounded Children, Healing Homes: How Traumatized Children Impact Adoptive and Foster Families* by Jayne Schooler, Betsy Keefer Smalley, and Timothy Callahan (2010) is a practical volume for parents of children who have a history of trauma and need help.
- *Raising a Secure Child: How Circle of Security Parenting Can Help You Nurture Your Child's Attachment, Emotional Resilience, and Freedom to Explore* by Kent Hoffman, Glen Cooper, Bert Powell, and Christine Benton (2017) focuses on the Circle of Security and how to be a secure base and safe haven for your children. This resource is particularly useful if your children have attachment issues.
- *Attaching through Love, Hugs, and Play: Simple Strategies to Help Build Connections with Your Child* by Deborah Gray (2014) can help you build attachment bonds with children who are struggling to do so.
- *The Out-of-Sync Child: Recognizing and Coping with Sensory Processing Disorder* by Carol Kranowitz (2006) offers excellent information for parents who have children with SPD.

A longer list of books appears in appendix A.

Conferences

At conferences you can learn new things and connect with like-minded people. Several conferences happen every year that are likely of interest to adoptive and foster families. I highlight two here.

The Refresh conferences bring together experts on the latest topics essential to effective adoptive and foster parenting. If you want the most up-to-date information for how to effectively walk alongside your child, Refresh is where you need to be—and after spending time among so many other adoptive and fostering families, you'll feel immensely supported, encouraged, and seen. The Christian Alliance for Orphans (CAFO) Summit gathers adoptive and foster parents, orphan advocates, pastors, and other leaders. Sessions cover topics such as effective adoptive and foster parenting, family preservation, and global orphan ministry. Lots of helpful resources are available for adoptive and foster parents specifically, as well as information about caring for vulnerable children more generally. A longer list of conferences appears in appendix B.

Training

Training sessions present education focused on a particular aspect of adoptive and foster parenting and are a great way to take a deep dive into a particular topic or work on specific parenting skills. Here I discuss two trainings intended to help parents who are working with kids who have experienced trauma in their background.

TBRI was developed at Texas Christian University under the direction of Dr. Karyn Purvis and Dr. David Cross. TBRI is an attachment-based, trauma-informed intervention designed to meet the needs of vulnerable children; trainings are for parents and professionals. There is a TBRI practitioner training for professionals. This training was a game-changer in my own therapeutic work with foster kids, and I highly recommend it. They also have online videos and DVDs for purchase.

Empowered to Connect, presented by Show Hope and the Karyn Purvis Institute of Child Development, is focused on TBRI principles. Empowered to Connect can be simulcast to your church, so no travel is required. Appendix C includes more information.

Websites

One especially helpful website for adoptive and foster parents is Confessions of an Adoptive Parent (ConfessionsOfAnAdoptive Parent.com). A big goal of this website is to provide hope and encouragement to adoptive and foster parents, but it also offers regular blog posts and podcasts to pass along helpful information about parenting and helping vulnerable children. Mike and Kristin Berry have been running this website for years, so most of your questions or the information you are looking for is probably there. The goals of Jason -JohnsonBlog.com are to encourage adoptive and foster families and to equip churches to help support vulnerable children and adoptive and foster parents. Two websites with resources for helping children with SPD are Out-Of-Sync-Child.com (the companion website for Carol Kranowitz's book) and SINetwork.org (which provides information and resources about SPD). Appendix D presents additional websites.

Professional Help and Coaching

Sometimes you find yourself in a tough situation, and you need some extra help. When this happens, it can be helpful to seek out a trauma-informed counselor to meet with your family. There are several things you can do to find a counselor for your family. First, one helpful way to find a counselor is through a personal referral. Ask around and see who other adoptive and foster families in your area have seen for counseling. Second, many foster and adoptive agencies have therapists on staff or have outside therapists they recommend. These agencies can be a helpful resource for getting a referral. Third, you can find a list of TBRI-trained practitioners here: https://child.tcu.edu/tbri-practitioner-list/ and https://showhope.org/support-for-the-journey/. Finally, you can search for a counselor on your own through websites such as Google or Psychology Today. Often counselors will have a website that describes their areas of specialization and approach to therapy. When you are searching for a counselor, ask if they have experience working with children impacted by adoption or foster care and be sure to ask if they are trauma-informed. If your child is dealing with a particular issue or limitation, ask if the counselor has experience working with your child's specific issue. One final note: Don't be afraid to "check out" a few counselors to find one you connect with. Counselors have a variety of personalities and approaches, and like any relationship, you won't connect with everyone. Keep at it until you find someone you like.

DEALING WITH LIMITED INFORMATION

When you don't know the specifics of your child's history with trauma, you may become frustrated because you're unsure of what help to seek. Sometimes it is a struggle to get a complete picture of your child's past. Sometimes this information may not be known. For example, you may have a sense that your child experienced abuse or neglect, but not know for sure. You may suspect that your child was substance-exposed in utero, but not know the specifics. This lack of information can be aggravating and is something that many adoptive and foster parents struggle with. There isn't an easy answer to this problem. You may never have full information about your child's difficulties and struggles, and there can be sadness and loss associated with the incomplete picture. As parents we are simply called to do our best. We gather the most and best information we can about our children and how to parent them. But in some situations and seasons we have to accept the limitations of our information and trust God to help us do the best we can with the resources we have.

EXERCISE: GETTING EDUCATED

Where are you in your adoptive or foster parenting journey around the education and information you have about parenting your child? What are your strengths in regard to information and education?

_____

_____

_____

_____

_____

_____

What are your areas of weakness or places where you might be able to grow? Where do you need more help and information?

_____

_____

_____

_____

_____

Consider your child's level of attachment and the three types of attachment: secure, anxious, and avoidant. What observations have you made about your child's attachment? What is one step you could take to help your child develop a more secure attachment?

_____

_____

_____

_____

_____

_____

Consider your child's history of trauma. Does your child have a history of abuse or neglect? What is one strategy from trauma-informed parenting that you could implement moving forward?

_____

_____

_____

_____

_____

_____

What resources have you found most helpful in your adoptive or foster care journey? What is one new resource you would like to try moving forward?

_____

_____

_____

_____

_____

_____

CHAPTER 6

The Water
Tangible Support

"'Whatever you did for one of the least of these brothers
and sisters of mine, you did for me.'"
—MATTHEW 25:40

IN THE LAST two chapters, we talked about the importance of good soil and sunlight. In this chapter, we discuss water—*tangible support*, which refers to practical aid or help, such as money, supplies, resources, and time for self-care. When you are connected to others through tangible support, you have opportunities for others to care for your children while you take care of you.

Sometimes we pay too little attention to our tangible needs—until we get to a place where meeting them gets too hard. People seem to assume that tangible needs will always be met—until they aren't. Psychologist Abraham Maslow (1943) described long ago why tangible needs are so important: without them, we can't move forward in our lives. In what's come to be known as Maslow's hierarchy of needs, our requirements as human beings build upon each other. Some needs (food, water, safety, belonging) are more basic or foundational than others (self-esteem, self-actualization). But you can't meet higher-level needs if the more foundational needs aren't in place. In the same way, it's difficult to thrive as an adoptive and foster family if your basic or tangible needs aren't being met on a regular basis.

DALIA

Dalia, age thirty-nine, worked in the local school district as a third-grade teacher. She had never married and had no biological children. She loved kids and had devoted her life to being an elementary school teacher. Dalia felt as if she had some gifts and talents for working with children, especially those who were struggling and needed extra love and attention. She also had always pictured herself being a mother and having her own kids, although over the years she had loosened her grip on her plan as she remained unmarried and hadn't started a family of her own.

Dalia began seriously considering becoming a foster parent. She grew up in El Paso and always had a heart for children in need. For example, she volunteered at her local Boys and Girls Clubs throughout college. After receiving her degree in elementary education, Dalia decided to take a lower-paying job in the city so that she could have more contact with kids who really needed her—and she was good at it. She had a knack for connecting with hard-to-reach children. Still, she agonized over the fostering decision. She worried about whether as a single mother she would be able to give a child the love and attention he deserved. She also worried about receiving judgments from her family, friends, and church community. They mostly encouraged her and were supportive, but some questioned whether her decision was a wise one. Someone at her church also questioned whether she could raise a child well without a father in the home.

Despite these obstacles, Dalia persisted, completed the licensing process, and was approved to be a foster parent. A couple weeks later, she was asked to take a sibling group—Jonathan (age three) and Sylvia (age one). Dalia was excited about taking them in but was also nervous about caring for two at once; the social worker with whom she was working, however, expressed some urgency about the situation. Jonathan and Sylvia's mother was homeless, and working out her living situation was going to take some time. The social worker explained that she was trying really hard to keep Jonathan and Sylvia together, and if Dalia wasn't able to take them, they would likely be separated.

Dalia agreed to taking both siblings, certainly an exciting time for her. Truthfully, though, she wasn't sure what to expect.

Some things about being a mom were awesome for Dalia. Overall, Jonathan and Sylvia were great kids. Jonathan had a lot of energy and was always exploring. Sylvia was a pleasant baby overall who loved being held and playing with blocks. Jonathan and Sylvia loved Dalia's dog, Riley, a border collie that was gentle and sweet with the children. The children had some trouble transitioning to Dalia's home, but all things considered, the change was fairly smooth. The kids had their share of angry outbursts, temper tantrums, and sleepless nights, which made sense given the circumstances. It was hard for Jonathan to understand foster care and why he couldn't see his mom or live with her. But they also had plenty of cuddles, "I love yous," and play time. The learning curve for parenting young children was steep, but Dalia was probably better prepared for it than most because of years working with young children.

Other elements of the transition were harder. One major challenge was financial. Dalia received a small amount of money from the state monthly to offset some of the costs, but it wasn't near enough to cover raising two small children. Just to prepare her home for Jonathan and Sylvia, Dalia had to purchase items—a crib, a small bed, a high chair, and much more—that took a large chunk out of her savings. As time went on, the money spent on food, clothes, diapers, and baby supplies added up.

Another major challenge was time. Before becoming a foster parent, Dalia was busy but she also had time for herself each week and lived a pretty balanced life. She had been involved in church, socialized with her girlfriends, and worked out two or three days per week at her local Y. Since becoming a foster parent, though, her free time had vanished. She seemed to have no margin whatsoever. Finding a babysitter to take both children was a challenge, and she didn't really have the money to pay a babysitter anyway. Plus, because the children were in foster care, finding a babysitter was more complicated. Taking a weekend away was out of the question, because the state had a rule that you couldn't leave a foster child with anyone for over twenty-four hours who wasn't also a licensed foster parent. This rule even applied to Dalia's extended family. The increasing demands on her time overwhelmed her. She was enjoying her time as a parent, but didn't really have any time for self-care. She wasn't so sure how long she could keep this up.

Dalia's story mirrors that of so many adoptive and foster parents. While emotional support is essential and life-giving, and informational support about attachment and trauma-informed parenting is necessary, those things don't matter without adequate levels of more tangible support in place. If you can't come up with enough money, food, and diapers, or if you have no time for self-care, those needs become your priority. Between the oxygen-mask example from the airplane and Maslow's needs hierarchy, you know by now what you need to do: take care of the basic needs, including yours, so that you are able to adequately care for yourself and your family.

In this chapter, I address two key aspects of tangible support: its main categories and how to find it. What kinds of tangible supports should you be thinking about? How can you tap into your community in order to help you meet your family's needs?

MAIN CATEGORIES OF TANGIBLE SUPPORT

Three key categories of tangible support to consider are financial, help with supplies, and time for self-care.

Financial Support

Talking about money can be uncomfortable, but we need to be honest about the financial realities that come along with adoption and foster care, especially when they are placed on top of your existing responsibilities. Finances are common stressors in most families, but especially in adoption and foster families. Money, though, offers a relatively easy opportunity for others to help meet the tangible needs of adoptive and foster families.

Adoption is expensive. If you have adopted or started down that road, you know this reality firsthand. For domestic and international adoptions, costs can begin around thirty thousand dollars and go as high as fifty thousand dollars, which is just for the adoption itself and doesn't include the postadoption expenses like therapy, medical bills, and all the supplies and furniture necessary to bring a child into the home. Foster care isn't as expensive as adoption, at least on the front end, but lots of expenses are still associated with preparing one's home to receive a child, such as readying a child's room. Some adoptive and foster families aren't adequately prepared for the financial burden, and even if they think they are, entering into the adoption and foster care journey changes and challenges the family's financial realities.

On the proactive end, an adoptive or fostering family could think about creative fundraising for support. For example, some families have hosted adoption fundraisers, held garage sales, or sent support letters to help with expenses. Families can apply for adoption grants at organizations such as Lifesong for Orphans, Show Hope, or Chosen and Dearly Loved. Both Hands is an organization that helps fund adoptions through helping to fix a widow's home. In addition to helping with the adoption fees, people in the community can also give financially to help with specific items, such as outfitting a child's room. Financial gifts could be used toward supplies and everyday items, such as diapers and even developmental toys or early reading books.

Dalia didn't realize how big the financial adjustment would be when she began foster care, and she realized pretty quickly that she needed to change her spending habits drastically. Before becoming a foster parent, she always had a bit of extra money for eating out, new clothes, and other expenditures. When she added the additional expenses of the children, all of that buffer was gone. Money soon became a constant source of stress.

Luckily, her church community had made a strong commitment to help Dalia financially. Her community had placed a strong value on caring for vulnerable children, and many of her friends and family were also involved deeply in what Dalia was doing. When Dalia was beginning to struggle financially, her community stepped in and was willing to divert some of their monthly tithes toward Dalia's family.

Supplies

As with biological families, adoptive and foster families need tangible supplies: crib, rocking chair, car seat, baby clothes, diapers, baby food, and toys for very young ones. Toddlers, older children, and teens all have their own sets of needs, and all come with costs (e.g. participating in extracurricular activities). Consider a teen's appetite, for example.

Communities and even families often don't think to provide an adoptive or foster family with the same celebrations as when a family has a biological child. With the latter, a nine-month period lends itself naturally to preparation and community participation. People can see the mother's belly grow, a more tangible element in itself. Community rites of passages take place, such as baby showers, that help the couple prepare for the baby. These rites of passage often don't happen for adoptive or foster families. Sometimes the community just doesn't think about it, or maybe they wonder if throwing a baby shower for an adoptive or foster family would be awkward. Also, adoptive or foster families might be told about their new placement with little or no warning, so there may not be enough time for the family to gather all the necessary supplies. In this situation, a community can really step up. Throw the parents a celebration, ask if they'd like to receive meals, or bring them a gift card to a local big-box store that they can use at their convenience for food, clothes, or something else they can buy in bulk. These seemingly small acts can be profoundly meaningful.

Some church communities have set up resource closets, where people inside the church and out can donate supplies such as toys, diapers, furniture, and clothes. Many local foster care agencies have resource closets as well. Families in need can pick up these items at the resource closet, which can operate similar to a food bank. Communities can also set up a calendar to bring meals to families. Churches could pair an adoptive or foster family with a support family who commits to helping with their needs for supplies throughout the year.

For Dalia, the resource closet at her local church was a much-needed source of tangible support. Dalia's community was very happy that she was embarking on this new journey, but they didn't think about throwing her a baby shower or asking whether she needed meals. Because Dalia was informed of her placement on short notice, and because she didn't know the age and gender of her foster children ahead of time, Dalia hadn't done a lot of shopping or specific home preparation. After the placement, Dalia was able to go to the resource closet and pick up baby clothes, diapers, and toys that enabled her to get started and provide Jonathan and Sylvia with a welcoming home right from the outset.

Time for Self-Care

Providing the opportunity for respite care and the chance for self-care may be the most important of all the types of tangible support that an adoptive or foster family needs, and it's the one that most often goes unmet. Many adoptive or foster families, and especially single parents, never get a day off. Finding respite care for a weekend away can be even more difficult because of state regulations.

Breaks and self-care are critical. However you give yourself some respite—reading, watching a movie, socializing, or going out for happy hour once per week—have structures in place so that you can continue to do so after you adopt or begin to foster. If you don't take these times to recharge, you might soon find yourself with a dead battery and at the end of your rope.

Self-care is also important in combating secondary trauma and compassion fatigue (Figley, 1995). Being in the trenches with our children and their trauma can have a significant impact on us. When a child you love so deeply has experienced something terrible and you hear these stories, you can experience emotional distress that can mimic posttraumatic stress disorder.

I remember doing therapy with a five-year-old girl who would process the details of the sexual abuse she experienced from an older adult. This little girl was so precious, and I felt so angry that she or any child could experience something so terrible. I remember shaking and crying in my car while driving home after she first shared her story with me. After getting home, I called a dear friend of mine to talk through what I experienced. I needed to connect with someone and talk through some of my feelings in order to take care of myself. Some of your kids have experienced incredibly sad, heartbreaking, and infuriating events. Give yourself space to grieve those experiences as well. Maybe you need to process your thoughts and feelings in an adoption or foster care support group, or with a safe and trusted friend or family member—or perhaps you need to pray, journal, and talk with God about it. Whatever works for you, you need time and space.

What are some practical ways to find time for self-care as an adoptive or foster parent? First, some foster agencies have licensed respite providers who can be used on a regular basis. Check with your local agency and see if that resource is available to you. Second, attending retreats and weekend getaways (e.g., Refresh, Rejuvenate or Deeply Loved for moms, Road Trip for dads) can be an excellent way to recharge and connect with like-minded folks. Third, be creative about finding ways throughout your day to recharge and take time for yourself. For example, could you find a gym that provides child care? Is your child interested in after-school activities that could provide you with an hour of time for yourself? Take advantage of these small moments for self-care throughout your day.

For Dalia, finding time for self-care was one of the toughest aspects about fostering. Although she was a busy full-time worker before she became a foster parent, she still had quite a bit of margin in her life and time for self-care. Dalia loved to read and was in a book club with several other women from church. She also enjoyed doing yoga for exercise and had several girlfriends with whom she would get together on a regular basis, going to movies or attending the latest concert that came to town.

Her time for self-care slowly diminished after Dalia became a parent. She took a break from the book club when she first brought Jonathan and Sylvia home. She meant to get back into it, but things were really busy and she wasn't sure if they were going to calm down in the future. Her energy was maxed out every day between work and taking care of the kids.

Dalia tried to continue socializing with her friends, but it was tough to find babysitters who felt comfortable taking both children. They weren't the most difficult, but Dalia felt like they needed a higher level of care than the typical high school babysitter. For a while, she tried to trade off babysitting with another family from church, but that didn't last. The other mom was polite about it, but Dalia came away with the feeling that Jonathan and Sylvia were putting too much of a strain on the other family.

One key turning point was finding others who were also engaged in adoption and foster care. These parents were more understanding of Dalia's situation because they were dealing with many of the same issues. Dalia befriended one family in particular who were foster parents but did not currently have a placement. They told Dalia that, at least for this season, they wanted to be her backup; they were committing to being with Dalia's family and providing regular respite care when she needed it. This development was huge for Dalia. She was able to go out at least once a month with her friends, and she even took a weekend trip to attend a friend's wedding. Dalia could drop off the kids for a couple hours while she did grocery shopping or caught up on housework. This reduced her stress, allowing her to reengage in some of her self-care activities, time that was critical for Dalia.

What can you do to refuel your tank? Next we discuss a step-by-step process for doing just that.

How to Get the Tangible Support You Need

So, how do we prioritize self-care, and how do we access resources for more tangible hands-on items? Perhaps you read the above, thinking, *I can't remember the last time I had time for myself.* Now that you have a sense of the kinds of tangible support that are available and what you might need, how can you put a plan in place to get the support you need on an ongoing basis? Remember that securing the support you need is a relationship investment you are making on behalf of your kids and that you'll need to revisit these sources of support over time.

Be Honest About Your Needs

Many adoptive and foster parents feel bad asking for help, having internalized a message that goes something like, *If I need to ask for help, it means I'm a failure or a bad parent.* This message couldn't be further from the truth. We all need help from time to time, especially when you are doing the challenging work of parenting children from hard places. Being honest about our needs and asking for help isn't something to be ashamed about; it's actually a courageous, honest, and humble act.

You know that you can't do this alone. You need other people by your side if your family is going to not only survive but thrive. Lay down your pride and the negative messages that come along with having needs. Be bold and ask for help. Don't apologize. You and your precious children are worth it.

Being honest about your needs is hard, especially if people have been judgmental or were telling you before you adopted or began fostering that this was a bad idea. You feel as though reaching out will open the gates for people to say, "We told you so." Many parents hear from family and friends, directly or indirectly, "You chose this," or "You shouldn't have done this if you couldn't handle it."

The reality is that some people in your life may be critical of your choices. But don't let the criticism of others take you off course from what God has called you to do. Seek out the people who will support and encourage you. Your health and the health of your children are too important—and reaching out doesn't make you a failure. Our children are beautiful and precious even in the midst of their messes—and so are you. You deserve to be supported. Let people come alongside you in your vulnerability to show you how loved you are.

What are some practical ways to ask for help? One idea is to reach out to your church for support. Churches often have pastors and volunteers who are tasked with meeting the needs of their congregants.

Set up a meeting with your pastor to discuss your needs and ask for support. For example, my church had an existing meals ministry to support people in need. We expanded the meals ministry to offer support to our foster and adoptive families. It was a gift for them to take a night off from cooking dinner while they juggled all their weekly appointments. A second idea is to be honest when friends and family ask how you are doing and if they can do anything to help. The common reaction to these questions is to say you're fine and move on. Instead, answer honestly. Put some of your needs out to trusted friends and family.

Admitting that she needed help was especially tough for Dalia. She had worked for years as an elementary school teacher, so she felt as if she should know what she was doing with young children who were struggling. Some people had judged her for being a single foster parent, and Dalia worried that asking for help would confirm their judgments that she just couldn't handle it. Dalia also felt bad about asking her friends for help, especially those who had full-time jobs. What right did she have to inconvenience other people just so she could get a break?

Dalia was eventually able to admit her need and desire for help. She had been floundering for quite some time when one of her friends had a tough conversation with her about the need to bring in more people to help her on a weekly basis. Talking with other foster parents to get a sense of their experiences also helped. When Dalia did so, she realized that her experience wasn't out of the ordinary; lots of foster parents needed extra help. And these parents were doing a great job and *still* needed help. While Dalia still sometimes felt bad about inconveniencing others and asking for help, as she did it more and more, it felt more comfortable. It was also an important lesson in humility (Worthington, Davis, & Hook, 2017). Dalia wasn't fully responsible for her kids' well-being. She needed her community, and she also needed God.

Build a Big and Diverse Team

Some adoptive and foster families make the mistake of asking one or two people for support, thinking that will be enough. A very small support team runs a much higher risk of burnout. Moreover, some children present with higher-than-average needs and challenges. As a result, providing respite care to give parents a break can sometimes be a big ask. Also, some families have limited financial resources for help and support. If you have a small number of people to turn to in times of need, these resources can be tapped quickly.

A better solution is to develop a large support team—the more people, the better. In this way, you are asking each individual or family to help only a small amount. That approach leads to less burnout and more support for you for the long haul.

You'll also want diversity in your support team. Get people on your team who are single, married without kids, and married with kids. Bring in people engaged in adoption and foster care themselves, as well as people who aren't. If you are a transracial family, recruit people to help who share your child's racial and ethnic background. Ask family and friends; solicit people from your church, work, and neighborhood communities. Different types of people have varieties of strengths and availabilities. A diverse support team gives you a greater chance of having someone available in the various times and situations who can help.

Dalia learned this lesson early on. When she first realized she needed more help, she joined a support group with other adoptive and foster families. This was an essential step in the right direction for her and her kids, and it was amazing to be in community with families like theirs. However, Dalia also realized that she needed a bigger support team, which would include families outside the adoption and fostering world with and without children. Sometimes when Dalia needed some tangible support, like a babysitter or respite care, she found that friends who were also engaged in adoption and foster care were pretty maxed out; they were often looking for support for themselves. When she broadened her support network, Dalia found a better chance of getting the support her family needed.

A word of caution: while diversifying your support team is healthy, be careful not to invite just anyone into your inner circle. Many people may love you deeply but not understand what you're experiencing. Take your time and be detailed before connecting on a deeper level with people. Ask questions about them and what they believe and know about adoption and foster care. Are they informed about trauma or attachment issues? Maybe share an honest story, without too many details, to see how they handle it. The people who hail you as a hero or call you an angel can backpedal quickly if your child does something extreme. Do your due diligence when building your community.

Have Support in Place before Your Placement

Many adoptive and foster families don't try to get support in place until it is too late. First, they make the mistake of thinking they can do it on their own. Then things start to get tough and they wait until they are almost completely submerged before reaching for a lifeline. Organizing support in this manner can cause problems. Sometimes you can't find the support you need if you haven't done the work ahead of time. Second, adoptive and foster parents can sometimes feel like they have failed or are bad parents when they've waited too long to find support, which can make the problem worse. Third, the kids can sometimes feel as if they are the source of the problem, which you don't want at all.

A better strategy is to develop your support team even before you adopt or receive your first foster placement. Know that you may need tangible support in regard to money, supplies, and time for self-care.

Consider your needs thoughtfully before your placement and figure out who or what can help you meet those needs.

With a broad-based system of support at the outset, you begin to establish a good rhythm of support. With such a system around you from the beginning, your children come to recognize these people as part of a relationship-focused extended family, not just people who swoop in when parents are in a bad place.

Some of you in the trenches might feel like you're in way over your head because you didn't know about forming the support first. It's *never* too late to reach out and ask for the support you need. Take stock and evaluate your most pressing needs, and reach out to your church and community to see who might be willing to join your team.

Prior to her foster placement, Dalia didn't think about having support in place. She thought she could probably do it on her own and access support when she needed it, but by the time she realized she needed help, she was really struggling, which meant she had to do the hard work of developing a support team in the midst of being in the trenches. For Dalia, the most important need was time for self-care. Eventually she reached out to her community and church and found some people she trusted who were interested in serving Dalia's family.

Stay Consistent with Tangible Support, Even If Things Seem Okay

Another pitfall for adoptive and foster families is only seeking tangible support in an emergency situation. In other words, they try to do things on their own until it gets really bad, and only then do they access their support team. For many reasons already discussed, this is a bad idea. Whether parents feel like failures or kids feel responsible, neither is true or a workable way to proceed. First, adoptive and foster parents often feel like they failed as parents when things get to a really bad place and they need to access support. Second, kids can also come to view accessing support as a sign that they did something bad (as opposed to support being viewed as a normal part of the routine). What's more, constant ups and downs in family functioning lead to stress, and the threat of "We told you so" becomes a hindrance.

For all these reasons, you should stay consistent with accessing support, even when things seem like they are going fine. Get in the habit of seeking tangible support from the very beginning, such as with babysitting and respite care. Your children should learn that parents need time for self-care. Bring your community in from the beginning and let other people pour energy and love into your children, even when things seem "better."

Dalia did a good job of keeping the support consistent once the team was in place. Her rotation of people was available for babysitting and respite care, and she developed the habit of taking time out for herself regularly. Dalia also had a babysitter come over once during the week so that she could concentrate on some of her most important errands. This was a lifesaver for Dalia and was also great for the kids. Lauren, a local college student, became one of the regulars for babysitting and helping. Jonathan and Sylvia developed a close relationship with Lauren and loved it when she came to babysit. Sometimes Jonathan would even ask Dalia when "La-La" would be coming over next to play with him. In this way, Jonathan and Sylvia began learning that they had many people in their life who loved and cared for them. In regard to financial support, some folks at church learned about some of Dalia's money challenges and said that they wanted to support her financially each month, similar to how a family might support a missionary. Dalia was thus able to benefit from regular, tangible financial support as well.

Give People the Opportunity to Support You

We've discussed the discomfort parents feel in asking for help. As an alternative, reframe your need for support as an opportunity for other people to get involved in the important work of looking after vulnerable children. Many people want to help others in some fashion and are seeking legitimate causes to receive their resources—time, money, and talents—and many people care deeply about helping vulnerable children. However, people may not know how to help or may be frustrated about giving to causes and not seeing a clear connection between their giving and the people they are trying to help.

Asking people for help gives them an opportunity to partner with God to serve the needs of vulnerable children. They can see clearly how their time, money, and resources are directly helping your child and family. For some people, helping your family may be the most meaningful part of their lives.

Dalia initially felt uncomfortable asking other people to help her family, but she soon was amazed at the positive responses. The people who joined her support team were blessing Dalia with their time, money, and resources, but they also told Dalia how much Dalia's family was blessing them. Some folks even developed a special place in their heart for vulnerable children and considered becoming foster parents themselves. Developing and maintaining a support team was a win-win for everyone involved.

Be Clear about Needs, Expectations, and Commitment

Once you have identified people you would like to ask for support, schedule a meeting with as many as you can gather together to get everyone on the same page. In this way, you can share more directly about your children, their struggles, and how best to respond to their needs. You may have to lay the groundwork to inform your support team about trauma and its impact, but take the time to do so. Giving your support system a clear understanding of how trauma has affected your children will help them better meet your children's needs and allow team members to be in it for the long haul. You can even invite your support system to trauma trainings with you, such as Empowered to Connect. If your team members are unwilling to consider undertaking such training, that reaction may speak to the level of support they would offer.

Discuss a game plan with your team and offer clear expectations. What sort of support will they be able to provide each month? One play date a month? One meal a month? Picking up and dropping off your kids at extracurricular activities? This may sound like a business meeting, but you can still keep it very personal. You are building relationships and community. Supporting our precious children is an important responsibility, and vigilance in that area is essential. Identifying clear expectations allows the support system to remain consistent and allows parents the freedom to receive that support. Additionally, because consistent support is so important, I recommend asking support systems for a tangible commitment to your family for a specific period of time (e.g., six to twelve months). After that time frame, connect again and discuss if they can continue making a commitment in supporting your family. Get in these rhythms with one another. You might even find some people or groups who want to operate on a six-months-on and six-months-off basis. Work with the best combination of opportunities you have.

Dalia learned over time that clarity about her family's needs and expectations for support was the best strategy. Early on in her foster care journey, Dalia would feel disappointed when her friends and family failed to support her and her children in the way she needed. Part of the problem, however, was that Dalia wasn't always clear about what help she needed. Being crystal clear about her family's needs also allowed her support team to be clear about what they were and were not willing and able to do to help meet Dalia's family's needs. Sometimes people could only help out a little bit, and that was okay. At least everyone was on the same page and knew the roles they'd be called on to fill.

EXERCISE: ACCESSING TANGIBLE SUPPORT

Where are you right now in regard to tangible support needs? What are your most pressing needs? Money? Supplies? Time for self-care? What other practical needs do you have?

_____

_____

_____

_____

_____

_____

Take stock of the tangibles you are receiving right now. Who is on your support team? How specifically are they helping your family?

_____

_____

_____

_____

_____

How comfortable do you feel asking for help and support? What gets in the way?

_____

_____

_____

_____

_____

_____

Write down the names of five people or families you could meet with to ask whether they might be interested in joining your support team.

_____

_____

_____

_____

_____

_____

How consistent is your support? Do you seek it on a consistent basis or only in an emergency?

_____

_____

_____

_____

_____

_____

What is one next step you could take to improve your family's level of tangible support?

_____

_____

_____

_____

_____

_____

SECTION 3

Support in Context

CHAPTER 7

How to Help without Hurting

You have not lived today until you have done something for someone who can never repay you.

—JOHN BUNYAN

IN THE FIRST section of the book, I talked about why support is so important for foster and adoptive families, kids as well as parents. I devoted the second section to a Replanted model that can help adoptive and foster families think about the types of support they need and how to get it.

In the book's final section, I shift gears and talk about how Christians and the church can come together to support adoptive and foster families in their journey. The church needs to be intentional about showing up in the lives of our adoptive and foster families. Michele Schneidler, cofounder of the nation's largest conference for foster and adoptive parents, sometimes encourages adoptive and foster parents by reminding them that they are "missionaries in their own homes." When they love and serve their children daily, parents' lives reflect the gospel of reconciliation. Adoptive and foster parents often find themselves in conversations in which people can't comprehend a lifetime commitment to a child who might have significant special needs or a temporary commitment to support a child's biological family when it was the source of abuse or neglect.

One unique challenge in this mission field is that there is no "sabbatical" and no "furlough," particularly in the case of adoption. Adoptive and foster parents don't get to return home for a season of rest before heading back into the mission field. The tragedy is that when the newness of the placement wears off, churches and communities often don't see the missionary aspect anymore, but rather another family with hard, dysregulated, misbehaved kids. Put simply, as Christians we can't acknowledge the important call to care for the orphan without showing up in the beauty and mess of the journey.

Maybe you have been reading this book and thinking, *I'd love to help adoptive and foster families, but I just don't know how,* or *How do I help without hurting? I don't know what that looks like and I feel completely unequipped.* If so, these next two chapters are for you. I want to equip and empower you to support foster and adoptive families well. Why? Because entering into the trenches and into someone's story can be hard. In a world of quick fixes, you want much more in your tool kit than often harmful phrases such as, "Pull yourself up by your bootstraps," or "God uses all things for his glory."

A young woman I know explained to me how both her parents were killed in an accident when she was a child. An aunt and uncle adopted her, but a few years later, that aunt died of cancer. Some years afterward, a woman from her church approached her and expressed how lucky she was to have had three mothers in the course of her life, as opposed to most individuals who have just one. Perhaps this comment was made with good intentions, but its insensitivity is apparent. This young woman had experienced the death of two mothers before the age of twenty-five; she felt far from lucky on that score. As Christians, we can be in such a hurry to offer hope, solutions, and positivity that we forget empathy entirely. Rushing past a family's pain and struggle can invalidate the family's very real situation. And unfortunately, not all helping is effective or even perceived that way.

Being informed and aware puts you in a position to make a positive impact on adoptive and foster families' lives. Prepped with information and awareness, individuals, churches, communities, and support groups are less likely to engage in avoidance, isolation, shutting down, or withdrawal. The church should never project those approaches onto our families. When this happens, adoptive and foster families hear the message that their story and their experiences are too big; they are all alone and need to figure out how to live on their own because they can't rely on others. The takeaway is that their personal family situation is too immense for even the kingdom of God to handle.

I remember talking with a foster mom about an experience she had with her parents. The two boys she had been caring for were reunified with their birth parents, and she was grieving. When she signed up to be a foster parent, she had always felt passionate about supporting reunification efforts when it was safe to do so, but now that the boys had left, she was grief-stricken. She was having a hard time getting out of bed, would break down in tears, and was in a place of deep sadness. Her parents came over one day to help her, and as she shared about the sadness she was feeling, her parents were at first supportive but eventually they started saying, "This is what you signed up for," a message that was not helpful for her at this time. Yes, she did sign up to be a foster parent, and yes, she still felt passionate about supporting reunification. But it's okay to hold both those things and still feel sad that those precious little boys won't be filling her home with their presence, laughter, stories, and memories.

In this chapter, I discuss how to effectively support adoptive and foster families through one-on-one relationships. In the next chapter, I talk more systematically about how a church community can set up an environment to help meet the needs of the congregation's adoptive and foster families.

Bailey and Mark

Bailey and Mark were married and in their late forties. Bailey worked part-time as a dental hygienist, and Mark worked as a history teacher at the local high school. They had three children. Grace, age twenty-five, had recently graduated college and gotten married; Danny, age twenty-one, was a senior at the state university studying engineering; and Blake, age sixteen, was a junior in high school. Bailey loved being a mom and had always had a heart for kids. She was a stay-at-home mom until Blake was in high school, and she had always enjoyed having the kids' friends over and getting to know them.

Bailey and Mark were in a transition period. Now that two of their kids were out of the house and their youngest had his driver's license, Bailey and Mark found themselves with some extra time on their hands. Having that time to themselves and to reconnect was fun, but lately they felt like they were ready to give back or serve in a more meaningful way. They had tried a few things at church, such as serving as ushers and greeters, but nothing seemed to click. At the same time, Bailey had been feeling sad about being "out of a job" as a mom, with her kids growing up and not needing her as much. Motherhood was part of her core identity, and she felt gifted at it. Bailey was trying to figure out what to do with those parts of herself now that her kids needed something different from her.

Bailey and Mark befriended a younger couple from church. Jason and Maria married in their late twenties and were now in their early thirties. They had been trying to start a family for a couple of years but hadn't gotten pregnant yet. Bailey and Mark were beginning to develop a closer relationship with Jason and Maria as the latter started seeing a fertility doctor. They took the process step by step, beginning with hormone treatments and ending with a try at in vitro fertilization (IVF). After IVF failed, the couple began to seriously consider whether God had another plan for their family, and they began to think and pray seriously about adoption. As they started the process, all the paperwork they had to complete and the abundance of questions they had to answer struck them. Included in those questions was a list of items about whether they were willing to take a child who had special needs, followed by a list of physical disabilities to which they could respond "yes" or "no." This process brought up so many emotions for them, as they felt like they were picking and choosing who they were willing to bring into their family. Imagine checking "yes" or "no" for a box that represents an actual child somewhere in the world. "Are you willing to adopt a child with HIV, cerebral palsy, a cleft palate, diabetes?" and so on. Every time they checked "no" felt like sending a rejection note to a child who needed a loving family. Bailey and Mark did their best to empathize with Jason and Maria, but sometimes they just didn't know what to say.

Jason and Maria eventually adopted a three-year-old from China named Linda. She was born with a cleft palate and would need to undergo surgeries as a result. Later, they adopted a second child from China named Kristi, who was HIV-positive. Kristi was six at the time of the adoption and had spent the majority of time in an orphanage. She seemed to have greater problems attaching to Jason and Maria than Linda. Both girls had a tough time with anxiety and struggled in school. They missed their friends at the orphanage. They had to learn a new language and adapt to life in America. It felt so different from what Linda and Kristi were used to. Sometimes Jason and Maria felt like they had extra full-time jobs trying to keep up with the girls' schoolwork, medical appointments, and anxiety and emotions. Jason and Maria were both maxing out their bandwidth.

Bailey and Mark walked through all of this with Jason and Maria. Mark and Bailey cared deeply for Jason, Maria, and their girls and wanted to help. One day at church, the pastor gave a talk about the call to care for orphans and vulnerable children, stressing that we all have a role to play, even if we aren't all called to personally adopt or foster. At lunch after church, Bailey told Mark that she wondered if God might be calling them to help Jason and Maria in a more consistent and intentional way with their time, money, and resources. Bailey had been wondering what she could do to serve with her mothering skills since her kids left the nest; maybe developing relationships and helping with Linda and Kristi was one way to continue to use her gifts.

As a result, Bailey and Mark committed to helping Jason and Maria consistently over time, a huge blessing for the parents and the girls. Jason and Maria had begun to realize that people who knew their daughter had HIV feared being around her, which broke their hearts. When Bailey and Mark intentionally stepped into their lives, Jason and Maria were so grateful that people could see their daughters for the beautiful, precious children they were. Bailey and Mark redirected some of their giving money each month to do something special for Jason, Maria, or the girls. They committed to play dates with the girls at least once a month, so that Jason and Maria could have a date or catch up on things they needed to do. Bailey also grabbed coffee with Maria periodically to check in and see how she was doing. Mark did the same with Jason. It was a beautiful picture of how one couple could support another in their adoption journey.

Some aspects of the support, however, were more difficult. Even though Bailey and Mark tried to understand and empathize, sometimes they didn't understand Jason and Maria's parenting. For example, Bailey believed it was important to provide children with love and support but balance that support with helping children take responsibility and develop their independence (e.g., Bailey would let her children "cry it out" before falling asleep). Maria, on the other hand, felt it was important to be extra-attentive to her children to help build their attachment relationship. Because there were so many children in the orphanage and only a few staff members, Maria knew many of her daughters' cries went unanswered. When Bailey and Mark would babysit the girls, Bailey would try her normal parenting techniques, which sometimes would result in the girls screaming and throwing a temper tantrum. One time they even had to call Jason and Maria home from their date to pick up the girls when things had reached a breaking point.

Bailey and Mark's more active role in trying to help Jason and Maria's family seemed at times to strain their friendship. Bailey was really trying to listen and be supportive for Maria, but sometimes she felt like Maria was just always complaining about the girls and how tough everything was. She felt that if Maria would change some of her parenting techniques, she would have a better outcome with the girls. But when Bailey tried to give Maria advice, Maria would get defensive and feel like Bailey was criticizing her parenting. One time Maria got angry and told Bailey she "just didn't get it."

As we can see from this example and others in the book, providing support for a family on the adoption or foster care journey can be challenging. Maybe you want to help and have tried to be supportive, but you're just not sure how best to do that, other than defaulting to your natural approaches. How can we help without hurting—from an informed, grace-filled, and aware place?

HELPING WITHOUT HURTING

To help answer this question I want to share six key encouragements for helping you learn how you can better walk alongside foster and adoptive families. These encouragements can keep you from the pitfalls people often stumble into when trying to provide help and support.

Encouragement #1: Lean In with Humility

When we think about assisting an adoptive or foster family, we don't always know where to start. We might see that a family is struggling. You want to help keep them afloat, but you're worried that your small piece of help won't do any good. The trauma that children who have been adopted or fostered have often experienced can seem overwhelming to you, and you might doubt your ability to interact with the child or help in any meaningful way. One common reaction when you feel overwhelmed is to back off and check out. A frustrating but common experience for adoptive and foster families is for help and support to stay in place for a few weeks and then begin to disappear when the reality of the situation or need becomes more apparent.

When you are feeling overwhelmed and feel like checking out, instead you should *lean in with humility*. Humility is key when trying to develop close relationships (Davis et al., 2013). Not knowing what to do is okay. Be humble and acknowledge your limitations. When you are feeling overwhelmed and uncertain about what would help, speak up and ask. The question, "How can I be a support to you and your family?" can be a lifesaver for adoptive and foster parents. Most families would be eager and delighted to hear such as question. Let them be the expert on their children, telling you what would be most helpful for them at that time.

Take the initiative to *educate yourself on adoption and foster care, attachment, and trauma-informed parenting*. Set aside some time to enter into their world and see if you can become better equipped to help and serve. Many adoptive and foster families have experienced the tremendous gift of a support network learning more about trauma and trying to understand the unique circumstances the family is facing. Getting educated sends the message that you see this family and you're in it with them for the long haul.

Recognize your limitations. This point goes along with humility, especially when you want to be all things for all people. However, jumping in the deep end, getting overwhelmed, and then vanishing is hurtful to the kids and the family. Take it slowly; get your toes wet. If providing respite care for a weekend seems like too much, be honest with yourself. Maybe you can provide respite care for one day or a few hours. Maybe if you don't feel comfortable taking full responsibility for a particular child, you could help out in a different way. Whatever level of support you are able to offer, do so with intentionality and consistency.

Bailey and Mark would occasionally feel overwhelmed with the high level of need of Jason, Maria, and their girls, and sometimes the girls' behavior seemed out of control. Since reverting to their own parenting styles was counterproductive if not harmful in this situation, Bailey and Mark had to acknowledge their own limitations. Simply asking, "How can I help?" became a way that Bailey and Mark could serve Jason and Maria's family without making assumptions about what that should look like. Bailey and Mark also attended local trauma trainings, which focused on trauma-informed parenting strategies. Afterward, Bailey and Mark better understood Linda's and Kristi's experiences in a deeper way, and Bailey had newfound respect for Jason and Maria's parenting.

Encouragement #2: Sit with the Pain and Offer Your Presence

One of the biggest problems people run into when trying to support adoptive and foster families is to give advice too quickly or try to fix the problem. Although the intention is good, several problems arise. It doesn't honor the struggle or pain and can feel invalidating to the recipient. When it comes to healing that needs to occur, whether a child's trauma or a broken marriage, the journey can be long. If the problem can be fixed, the solution will likely involve gradual progress over time. There often is no quick fix, which is just one reason your advice or solution will likely be perceived as not helpful. Also, the family you are trying to help has probably already received plenty of advice, including yours. They might even have tried some of it, but more than advice is obviously needed.

What's more, giving advice or trying to fix the problem often puts you in a one-up position over the person you are trying to help. "I have the answers and you don't" makes the relationship hierarchical. What is needed instead is for you to simply *be with* the person or family you are supporting.

Being with those you love in their pain and offering your presence can be a beautiful gift. You'll likely need coping skills of your own for the anxiety you feel when you see someone hurting. You'll also need humility—to admit that you don't have all the answers, and that there are some problems you don't have the power to fix. Simply sitting with a person or family in their pain—and just being with them while walking through life—can be incredibly healing. In a way, I believe God takes this same action with and for us. God doesn't promise that we will live an easy life without trouble (John 16:33), but God does promise that nothing can separate us from his love (Romans 8:38–39). In other words, God offers us his presence, always.

Bailey had a tough time seeing Maria and her girls hurting and in pain. She felt a strong pull to do something to help, but at the start of their friendship, this aid often came across as giving advice or trying to be the fixer. Maria often felt like Bailey rushed too soon to give advice or offer a solution before taking the time to understand what life was like for Maria and her family. At one point, when Bailey was in the midst of offering some of her advice, Maria started to cry. She was struggling and feeling alone, and a lecture just wasn't what she needed. To Bailey's credit, she recognized that something was wrong and stopped to ask Maria what she was feeling. Maria was able to share with Bailey that sometimes her tendency to give advice and try to offer a quick solution was actually more hurtful than helpful. Bailey asked Maria what she needed, and Maria was able to share that, more than anything, she just needed someone to be there and to listen. More than anything, Maria needed Bailey's presence.

Encouragement #3: Offer Grace

Judgments and criticisms are common in the parenting world, maybe especially in the adoption and foster care arena. Everyone—even children—has ideas about what parenting should look like. Nothing, however, derails emotional support and safety like judgment and criticism (J. P. Hook et al., 2017). When we judge and criticize another human being, we can't love (Boyd, 2004); the two reactions are mutually exclusive. If we want to truly support adoptive or foster families, we have to stop the judgment and criticism.

Grace—unconditional acceptance—is the antidote to judgment and criticism. Grace is based in our relationship with God, who loved us and sent his son, Jesus, to die for us, even though we were stuck in sin and shame. God didn't wait until we were deserving or had achieved a certain standard of good behavior. He reached out with grace, love, and acceptance *first*. Grace isn't based on anything we did; it is a free gift (Ephesians 2:8–9). In the same way, we are called to offer grace to each other, even if the other person may not deserve it.

How do we offer grace? One key way is to be consistent in our love, acceptance, and presence, even if the situation or context changes. Grace means that we might develop a relationship with someone and help support that person even though they can't necessarily repay us in any traditionally equitable manner. If a person does something of which we disapprove, grace means that we don't abandon the person or relationship. Grace means that if someone does something that hurts or offends us, we forgive instead of taking revenge.

When offering grace with parents, remember their fear that their children will also experience judgment, criticism, and rejection, especially if they have disorders that cause extreme behaviors. The ability to love a child unconditionally, in spite of the child's behaviors, is a major gift for parents and kids.

Exploring the contrast between judgment and criticism on one hand, and grace on the other hand, was a key turning point for Bailey and Mark in their relationship with Jason, Maria, and the girls. In the beginning, Bailey and Mark would sometimes find themselves criticizing Jason and Maria for their parenting techniques or interactions with Linda and Kristi. They would try to frame their criticism as a question or as helping, but the criticism came through loud and clear.

The key shift for Bailey and Mark was recognizing that they also had hard times and were in need of grace. They had problems and rough edges too. Bailey was sometimes too mean to her friends and family with her criticism. She had even lost friendships because of it. Mark had problems with anger management. He would occasionally lose his temper and yell at Bailey or his kids. Bailey and Mark were just like Maria and Jason: they needed grace from God, their friends, and their family. If Bailey and Mark needed grace, why shouldn't they offer the same to Jason and Maria?

Encouragement #4: Support the Parents and the Kids

Admittedly, much of this book has spoken to the parents. Part of this is pragmatic: adults read books like this, and ten-year-old kids generally don't. But when you think about being with and looking after adoptive and foster families, think specifically about supporting the kids too. Building independent relationships with them is just as important. A research study from Harvard's Center on the Developing Child (2017) concluded that the most important factor for children to develop the capacity to overcome serious difficulty and hardship is having at least one stable and committed relationship with a supportive adult. Many kids who have been adopted or fostered have experienced ruptures in trust, relationships, and love. Even outside their biological family, children may also have experienced the hurt and abandonment of a support system that initially showed up but has slowly vanished over time. We never want to reaffirm those messages, which can damage a child's ability to develop loving, trusting relationships. We want the children impacted by adoption or foster care we know to understand that we are on this journey with them—unconditionally. Additionally, every child should know how deeply beautiful they are—that their messes are never too big for us and never call their preciousness and worth into question. You can have an unimaginable impact in one child's life, and it's all about *relationship*. Developing a deep, trusting relationship with a child takes time and commitment but can drastically impact the trajectory of the child's life and yours.

What does supporting a child or teen look like? First, as you would do with parents, *ask them*. Find out what they enjoy doing. A grad school professor I had for developmental psychology discussed the importance of staying current with what kids are into these days—the most popular TV shows, games, toys for kids, and music. Kids themselves are your best teachers. Just ask; they'll tell you.

Second, *do what they enjoy with them*. Don't just be a bystander, but be actively engaged and connected. If they want to play with dolls, get down on the floor with them. Don't just sit there and say, "That's nice." An eight-year-old boy I counseled who was in foster care was really into playing basketball. Each time we met for counseling, we'd head outside to the basketball court and shoot hoops. Engaging in that activity allowed us to develop rapport, have meaningful conversations, and ultimately have fun. Third, *be consistent*. Remember, you're developing a relationship, which takes time and consistency. Make plans to engage weekly or monthly in the activity of their choosing. Before you leave them, make sure you've found another time on the calendar to connect, showing the kids this was not a one-and-done experience.

Fourth, *provide contexts for children to develop relationships with other children impacted by adoption or foster care.* That way, kids can have their own "me too" moments and not feel alone. Adoption and foster care support groups can be a great place for kids to connect.

Bailey and Mark paid special attention to Linda and Kristi from the beginning. They tried to learn about each girl's preferences. They made a point to get down on the girls' level and be with them each time they got together. They also committed to taking the girls on monthly play dates, which also gave Jason and Maria some time for self-care. Bailey and Mark always acknowledged holidays and birthdays, giving Linda and Kristi something special and keeping them involved. In this way, not only did Jason and Maria receive support but Linda and Kristi felt loved and supported also.

Encouragement #5: Learn Your Limits, Start Small, and Be Consistent

Sometimes people get really excited and energized about helping and supporting an adoptive or foster family. This kind of enthusiasm is a good thing, and I certainly don't want to dissuade anyone from jumping in and helping. Our adoptive and foster families need people who are excited and energetic.

The problem is that excitement and energy don't always last. Before committing too much, consider your own limits and prior commitments. Time and time again, adoptive and foster families have someone who starts off so happy and supportive, but the excitement and the support dwindle in a few short weeks. An adoptive dad shared that he received many promises from people who wanted to support his family, and he believed every one of the promises and people were sincere. Unfortunately, within three months, 90 percent of the support had stopped. Adoptive and foster families need consistent, long-haul help and support. Support that drops off after a short time hurts kids too, when they're already dealing with abandonment issues.

The antidote to giving too much and then quitting consists of these simple steps.

- *Know your limits regarding time, money, and emotional and other resources.* Before you commit, think about what support is realistic for you to offer. Talk to your spouse and kids, if you have them, about your limits as a family. If you understand your limits, you are more likely to help in a sustainable way over time.
- *Start small.* Sometimes when starting something new, we bite off more than we can chew, overpromising and underdelivering. Unfortunately, we often can't keep the pace we began with, and so we quit in frustration. A better idea is to start small, with something that you know you can sustain over time. As time goes on, if you want to increase your commitment, that's fine, as long as you always keep your capabilities in mind.
- *Be consistent.* Small efforts done consistently over a long period of time can make a huge difference. When you come to join with an adoptive or foster family, try to stick with it for the long term; the benefits will flow both ways.

When they first started to develop a relationship with Jason and Maria, Bailey and Mark tried to do too much too soon. Eventually, they realized they were getting burned out and were able to have an honest conversation with Jason and Maria about their limits. Jason and Maria appreciated Bailey and Mark for being honest with them, and they worked out a different pace for helping and getting together that Bailey and Mark felt was more manageable.

Because they recognized their limits, Bailey and Mark were better prepared for the long term. They were committed to developing relationships with Jason and Maria and also with their daughters. Bailey and Mark's kids were also excited about continuing to get together with Jason, Maria, and the girls when they were back in town visiting. Bailey and Mark hoped to continue going through life with Jason and Maria for a long time to come.

ENCOURAGEMENT #6: BE SPECIFIC

Sometimes when people offer to help foster and adoptive families, they are vague in their offer. For example, someone might hear that a family is in a challenging season, and say something like, "I'd love to bring you a meal sometime—let me know when you need it." It's hard (and sometimes awkward) for foster and adoptive families to follow up on the offer, and it may not happen. Instead, be specific and direct about the support you are hoping to offer. For example, "I'd love to bring you a meal this week. What's your favorite restaurant? What day is best—Monday, Tuesday, Wednesday, or Friday?" Make it as easy as possible for the family to accept your help.

Early on in their relationship with Jason and Maria, Bailey and Mark would make vague comments about wanting to help. Bailey would see Maria at church and say, "We'd love to babysit sometime—let us know what works for you." Maria would say thanks in the moment, but the reality was that her life was so busy she often forgot about it. And sometimes she felt bad about reaching out and asking them to babysit. It was more effective for Bailey to give Maria a call and say, "We'd love to babysit the kids so you and Jason can have a date night this weekend. We're free Friday or Saturday night—would either of those nights work well for you?" Maria very much appreciated that Bailey was specific and direct—Maria could respond accordingly and they could actually make something happen.

EXERCISE: HELPING WITHOUT HURTING

Where are you in your journey of helping support adoptive or foster families in your community? Who are you in relationship with? How has God spoken to your heart in regard to supporting adoptive and foster families?

_____

_____

_____

_____

_____

_____

Reflect on ways you have tried to help adoptive and foster families but may have inadvertently done some harm.

_____

_____

_____

_____

_____

_____

How could you try to help with humility? What questions, from a position of humility, do you have for the adoptive or foster family you hope to support?

_____

_____

_____

_____

_____

What comes up for you when you see an adoptive or foster family hurting? What is it like when you just sit with a person going through a difficult time? Is it hard for you to hold back from giving advice or trying to fix the problem?

_____

_____

_____

_____

_____

Are you able to give grace—unconditional acceptance—rather than judgment or criticism? If offering grace is difficult for you, think about an area of your life where you need grace for yourself. Could you in turn offer grace to an adoptive or foster family in your community?

_____

_____

_____

_____

_____

_____

What are your limits—time, money, emotional, and resources—when you think about helping adoptive and foster families? Are you able to honestly consider your limits and then stay within them?

_____

_____

_____

_____

_____

_____

_____

What would be one small, specific step you could take to help an adoptive or foster family in your community? Could you commit to helping with this small step consistently over time? How long might you want to make a commitment to help, before reevaluating?

_____

_____

_____

_____

_____

_____

CHAPTER 8

Support through the Church

Prayer in action is love, and love in action is service.
—MOTHER TERESA

W E'VE BEEN DISCUSSING individual relationships. Now let's look at one's broader community—specifically, the local church. When I worked as a therapist for kids in foster care, regularly meeting with struggling families, one of my big questions was, where was the church in all of this? Many of my families were committed Christians who attended church regularly. I thought the church would be a perfect source of help and support, but almost none of my families received any kind of meaningful help and support from their congregations.

I'm a big believer in the power of the local church. I grew up in the church, and it has played an important role in shaping the person I am today. The same goes for my husband, Josh, and my other coauthor, Mike. We all love the church, yet we all realize that the church has been a place of hurt and pain for many foster and adoptive families. Shouldn't we expect the opposite?

Unfortunately, I think local churches in general are not fulfilling their potential when it comes to supporting adoptive and foster families. Many of our churches would wholeheartedly agree that the cause of the fatherless is deeply important to the heart of God. Many churches even encourage families to explore whether God is calling them to foster or adopt. However, far fewer churches truly show up as that calling plays out among their congregants.

While the church should be the one place where people can come

no matter what—for love, acceptance, support, and encouragement—some people view churches as unsafe spaces for their adoptive or foster families. Messages—direct and indirect—may include,
"We just are not equipped enough to meet his needs in Sunday
school," or "We'd love to have a ministry for adoptive and foster
families, but the money just isn't there in the budget."

Much of this hurt hasn't been intentional. The church is full of
well-meaning folks who care about vulnerable children. But local
churches lack knowledge in developing comprehensive programs
and ministries to truly meet the needs of adoptive and foster families. Given these conditions, how can the church be a source of
support for our families? How can we empower the local church and
local leaders to support our families? What does a practical application for local church support look like? We answer based on some
of our experiences gained through Replanted, a support ministry for
adoptive and foster families.

THE BARRIERS

Churches are complex organizations with great potential, yet they
often miss the mark in helping adoptive and foster families. I see
five key barriers that hold local churches back from being places of
love and support for our families.

Limited Resources

With competing demands on top of limited resources, the needs
in a church's congregation and community can never be fulfilled
completely. Church leaders and congregants have different priorities
and goals, individually and collectively. Some church leaders may
set a vision for the church that doesn't necessarily prioritize caring
for vulnerable children. When church leaders are deciding where to

place their limited resources, postplacement support for vulnerable children might take a backseat unless the church's mission specifically addresses it.

Lack of Knowledge

Local churches institutionally lack knowledge and information about how to support adoptive and foster families. That was one of the primary motivations for this book: to help churches meet the particular needs of adoptive and foster families in a meaningful way. Without adequate knowledge of what adoptive and foster families face—and an understanding of what could help families in a cost-effective way—churches often throw in the towel, believing that professional therapists are better suited to the task.

Failure to See and Care for Struggling People

Local churches are not often at the forefront of helping people in poverty or with mental illness—that is, people whose lives contain a great deal of struggle. Adoptive and foster families sometimes present with a high level of need, and many churches are unprepared for it. Local churches are so often homogeneous, and people who come through the door looking or acting different makes people uncomfortable. Many churches quite simply don't meet people's needs at a deep level. That takes a lot of work—and can feel overwhelming.

Lack of Critical Mass

Sometimes a church lacks a critical mass of foster or adoptive families, so they decide to do nothing. Smaller churches especially may only have a handful of adoptive or foster families. If you are part of a group not highly represented in a church, sometimes you can feel like the church has forgotten you. Many adoptive and foster families feel easily overlooked, which is unfortunate yet not hard to change.

198 | *Support in Context*

Lack of Innovation

Postplacement support can require nontraditional ways of thinking and serving. Many local churches do things a certain way, resisting change and outside-the-box thinking. I remember speaking with a woman who was part of her church's leadership team, and she was trying to get the pastoral staff to increase support for foster and adoptive families. She invited them to attend two days of trauma training specifically designed for those caring for or supporting children impacted by adoption or foster care. The response from church leadership was resistant and nonsupportive, essentially, "We aren't into this New Age stuff. We do things the traditional way."

An investigation by Lifeway Research (2018) illustrated some of these issues. In a study on how churches engaged with adoption and foster care, a growing number of churches have members who are fostering and adopting. Furthermore, a growing number of church leaders have encouraged church members to adopt and foster. Such developments are certainly positive. However, few churches provided postplacement support for families engaged in adoption and foster care. That's the key problem in a nutshell: *churches are quick to discuss the orphan care crisis and encourage church membership to adopt and foster, but churches bow out when it comes to caring for families after they adopt and foster.*

HOW CAN THE CHURCH SUPPORT ADOPTIVE AND FOSTER FAMILIES?

Here I outline six principles for how the church can help support adoptive and foster families. These principles are based on my experiences as a therapist in the foster care system, as well as leading a national support ministry for adoptive and foster families. If churches would prioritize these principles, I believe that the church could become a safe place for effectively meeting the needs of children and their families.

Principle #1: Provide Presupport and Postsupport

As I discussed in chapter 3, caring for vulnerable children is deeply biblical. I have yet to meet a pastor who thought caring for vulnerable children was misguided or unbiblical. Unfortunately, *many sermons that talk about orphan care focus on encouraging people to adopt or foster but do little to focus on those who are already doing so.* In other words, most energy in church is spent on what happens *before* a family brings a child into their home. Considerably less time, energy, and resources are given to what happens after a family adopts or fosters, which is a shame, because this lack of support leaves families more or less on their own and can ultimately lead to family breakdown and failed placements.

Also, "convincing" someone they want to adopt or foster is relatively easy. Sometimes all it takes is a well-crafted sermon and a strong emotional appeal. But supporting an adoptive or foster family through all the ups and downs of raising kids is much more difficult, and churches don't want the responsibility. Supporting families for the long haul takes a large investment of time, money, and resources. People need to step outside of their comfort zone and be with hurting families. It might force churchgoers to rethink what being a successful family or a good kid looks like. Support of adoptive and foster families isn't just a checklist item.

Investment in families after the placement is absolutely essential, which may mean a paradigm shift for how churches think about adoption and foster care. Churches need less "convincing" Christians to adopt and foster and much more support and encouragement after a family adopts or fosters. For example, when Replanted first started, it was important for us to develop support for foster and adoptive families first, before encouraging prospective families to foster or adopt. We believed that encouraging families to adopt or foster without having support in place would set families up for failure. If the church truly prioritizes caring for vulnerable children, we have to provide postplacement support to adoptive and foster families. Moreover, families who see the church openly and actively supporting adoptive and foster families may feel more encouraged to explore it knowing that their needs would be met.

Principle #2: Don't Just Talk the Talk; Walk the Walk

This principle builds on the first but should be made explicitly. Providing verbal support and encouragement is a good start, but if tangible support doesn't follow in the form of money, resources, and ministry support, the verbal support often comes across as empty.

Jesus had a lot to say about loving and serving people with our actions and behaviors. When an expert in the religious law asked Jesus to clarify what it meant to love one's neighbor, Jesus told the parable of the Good Samaritan (Luke 10:25–37). The Good Samaritan didn't just "love" with words the man who was attacked by robbers, he loved him with his money and actions. The Good Samaritan met the man's needs, and Jesus said we should do likewise. Jesus said that when we meet the needs of the "least of these"—when we provide food, water, shelter, and clothing; look after the sick; visit those in prison—we are actually loving God himself (Matthew 25:34–40). The focus is on right action. Talk is cheap.

In the same way, churches who support adoptive and foster families with their words but not their actions are avoiding the hard work Jesus called us to do to love and care for vulnerable children and their families. Loving and supporting as Jesus commanded means action: time, money, and resources for ministries that support adoptive and foster families preplacement and postplacement.

Principle #3: Partner to Support Adoptive and Foster Families

Sometimes churches don't meet the needs of adoptive and foster families because they may just have a few in the congregation. Thus, not enough demand might be present to set up entire ministries to meet the needs that adoptive and foster families bring. In these situations, churches can partner with other churches or community ministries to provide support.

This approach has been at the heart of the Replanted ministry and model to help support adoptive and foster families. One great thing about the call to care for vulnerable children is that it crosses denominational lines. Looking after the orphan is deeply biblical, not a conservative or liberal issue. It's not about a single church or denomination. It's about the entire Christian church coming together to help meet the needs of vulnerable children and their families.

So many things divide churches nowadays. All Christians agree on very little, if anything. The call to care for vulnerable children, however, is a unifying cause all Christians can support. In this way, the call to care for vulnerable children could help churches across the liberal/conservative spectrum work together to meet a pressing and urgent need.

Churches can unify, working together to help meet local needs. Are there not enough adoptive and foster families in your congregation to start or support a small group ministry or resource closet? Partner with the church across the street and see if you can meet the needs of families in both your communities. Maybe you have something they don't, and vice versa (for example, financial resources vs. a large volunteer pool). Also, there might already be a ministry focused on adoptive and foster families in your community (e.g., a Replanted ministry) that you could partner with and support, or you could partner with the churches in your area to start one. The burden doesn't have to solely fall on your or any one church alone, but together local churches can collectively help create an infrastructure to support adoptive and foster families: a beautiful reflection of the church.

Principle #4: Become Trauma-Informed

Most churches, as well as the employees who work for them, don't understand trauma or the impact trauma has on kids and families. Because of this lack of knowledge and information, church staff and volunteers can often be insensitive and sometimes even cause harm toward kids and their families. This lack of trauma-informed care sends a shameful message to a child with trauma.

Local churches need to prioritize education and information about trauma and encourage—perhaps require—all church employees and volunteers to attend training on the effects of trauma on children, as well as how to engage with kids impacted by adoption or foster care in a trauma-informed way. What a way to enter into the post-placement support journey in a tangible way. Instead of sending the message that the church can't meet the needs of your child, we send the message that your child and family are so important to us that we are going to become trauma-informed so that your child is always safe and cared for by this church. This small step would hopefully minimize much of the hurt and pain that churches inadvertently cause adoptive and foster families.

Judy and Max were new foster parents of a seven-year-old child named Rogers. They were members of the church and well-integrated into the church community. After they brought Rogers home, Judy and Max figured they would continue to attend church and help integrate him into the church and Sunday school program. However, like Sara from chapter 1, Rogers was initially rejected from Sunday school when his behaviors proved too much for his teachers to manage.

Rogers struggled to adjust. Part of the difficulty had to do with his trauma background and history of abandonment. He had trouble trusting new people, which included his new foster parents, but especially strangers. He didn't engage in the Sunday school program, and he sometimes would act out in an aggressive way toward the teachers and other students.

The Sunday school teachers didn't really understand Rogers's history, and they also didn't have any understanding of trauma and its impact on children's behavior and emotions. They simply viewed him as disobedient. The Sunday school program was also very structured, and there wasn't much flexibility for a kid to do something different from the general program activities. For example, Judy and Max tried to teach the Sunday school teachers some things they could do if Rogers started to feel overwhelmed, in order to help him relax and self-soothe. His teachers were open to these suggestions initially, but they didn't really make it a priority to give Rogers the extra time, attention, and energy he needed to integrate into the program. After Rogers acted out again and pushed a fellow student, the pastor in charge of the church's youth activities sat down with Judy and Max and said that one of them would have to stay with Rogers from now on.

Once this issue was brought to the attention of the church leadership, they tried to take steps to make sure the church workers and volunteers had a better understanding of trauma. For example, during a staff meeting, they brought in a licensed professional counselor who worked with troubled kids to do a training on trauma and its effects on the brain. The speaker was so well-received by the staff that they brought her back to give the same talk at the new volunteer training orientation. Little by little, the staff and volunteers at this church were becoming better informed and trained about trauma, which had a positive impact on kids in the congregation who were adopted or currently in foster care, as well as their families.

Principle #5: Listen to the People Involved in the Work

Humility, which involves having an awareness of your limitations and being open to other perspectives (Worthington, Davis, & Hook, 2017), can be difficult to practice. We all want to think of ourselves as wise and knowledgeable, so admitting we don't know something or need help can be a challenge. Humility can be especially difficult for churches and leaders who are placed in positions of power and authority over religious and spiritual matters (Hook et al., 2015). However, when churches and religious leaders assume that they know more about supporting the needs of adoptive and foster families than they actually do, families can get hurt and needs often go unmet.

A better strategy for a local church is to admit its limitations regarding what they know about supporting adoptive and foster families and be open to listening to the actual adoptive and foster families themselves, as well as trained professionals with specific expertise, such as counselors and social workers. The result should be an open dialogue with the goal of listening and learning. It also means being willing to share power with others rather than asserting oneself as the expert on all matters related to adoption and foster care. This involves listening to the voices of women in contexts that are often patriarchal (James, 2015), because women often play important roles in caring for children and families.

Principle #6: Lead with Grace

Of everywhere on earth, the church should be the one place where people know beyond any doubt that they will experience unconditional love, mercy, and grace—where people feel loved and accepted, just as they are, even if they are struggling intensely. The church should model the love and grace of God, who loved us first, even while we were still sinners (Romans 5:8).

Unfortunately, people often do not experience grace when they come to church; sometimes the exact opposite happens. A lack of grace can be communicated explicitly, such as when church leaders or members judge or criticize certain groups of people. But a lack of grace can often be communicated implicitly too. For example, church leaders and members might not share their troubles, instead trying to put their best foot forward. When this happens, the implicit message is that you are not welcome if you are really in a dark place.

Another way that a lack of grace is communicated implicitly is the heavy focus many churches place on right behavior and action. You might be saved by grace, but now you're in the process of sanctification, so you need to get your act together. When the focus becomes right behavior and right action, people struggling to improve their actions and behaviors, like many kids and families impacted by adoption or foster care, may feel rejected.

Still another way that a lack of grace can be communicated implicitly is through the church's focus on appearances. When everyone dresses up for church and the pastor wears fancy robes in front of the congregation, the implicit message is that you must present a particular image in order to come to worship and meet with God. *But what will people think of me if I show up to church as I really am, with my messy hair and stained shirt? Will my child in foster care be shown grace if he has a bathroom accident and messes up the buttoned-up, holy image that the church is trying to portray?* Sadly, in many churches, adoptive and foster families find out that the answer to the second question is no.

An adoptive mom at a conference was sharing her story, completely and authentically. At one point, she explained that if the people in her community and her church really knew the struggles her family was going through, they would think she was such a fraud.

"Fraud"—it's a powerful word and a sad reality, that an adoptive mom would feel like she cannot be honest about her journey because she needs to put forth that she's doing okay and has it all together.

The alternative is to focus on grace from beginning to end and actually engage all congregants with grace on a daily basis. Focus on grace from the pulpit—every weekend. Celebrate vulnerability rather than having one's act together. Prioritize loving God and loving others over following rules for right action and right behavior. Let your hair down, show up as you normally live your life, and invite your congregants to do the same. When in doubt, give people a break. As Ian Maclaren said, "Be kind, for everyone you meet is fighting a hard battle."

WHAT ABOUT THE BIRTH PARENTS?

Up until now, we've focused almost entirely on supporting foster and adoptive families and their children. However, we have not yet addressed another key voice: the birth parents. A growing number of domestic adoptions in the United States are open (55%), meaning the adoptive and birth family know each other and have ongoing contact (Wetzstein, 2012). If we are to care for the cause of the fatherless, we must support birth parents as well. To love our children well means we love their first family also. Whether it is a birth parent who has created an adoption plan for a child, or a birth parent who is trying to reunify with a child in the foster care system, caring for and supporting birth parents is incredibly important.

We tend to villainize birth parents, or perhaps they make us feel threatened or uncomfortable. Especially in foster care situations, loving and supporting birth parents can be hard. You may have thoughts like, *How could they harm their child or let someone harm their child, or choose to continue using drugs while pregnant, or fail to provide food, shelter, and safety?* I can relate. When I was in graduate school, our ethics professor asked us which type of client we'd have a hard time sitting with in a room together. That question was easy for me to answer: people who had abused or neglected their children. I couldn't even fathom sitting in a room with someone who did so, let alone give them grace and journey with them in their healing process.

Fast-forward two years, and that is exactly what I was doing. In addition to counseling kids in foster care, I was sitting across from birth parents in the counseling room. During this process, something unique happened to me. I began hearing story after story from birth parents who were hurting in their own unique ways—and the parents' own experiences of abuse, foster care, abandonment, grief and loss, death, and substance abuse. Now I want to be clear, being hurt themselves doesn't excuse their role in what happened to their children, of course, but I found that instead of villainizing them, I was empathizing. The birth parents were people too, broken and hurting. I could choose to judge them, but I had things they didn't. I had a healthy family and support network around me, and I had my faith. My heart shifted from judgment to grace.

I sat with many parents in the foster care system who were trying to reunify with their children and felt like they had no healthy support system around them. For the most part, that was true. One father shared with me that he started using drugs with his parents when he was ten years old. Drugs became a normal part of their family life, and all throughout his teen years he abused substances with his mother. But his substance abuse had another backstory. His mother was also prostituting herself to make ends meet. He recalled traumatic memories of times these men would physically abuse him. He was using substances as a way to cope. His story was heartbreaking.

When hearing about his past, though, I was not surprised that things played out the way they did. He desperately wanted to be a safe and loving parent for his daughter, but he needed to experience a lot of healing in order to do so. In the same way we say to a child, "I see you in the mess of your trauma and I'm going to walk alongside you through it," we can give this same message to birth parents, regardless of whether they are able to parent their children or not.

Another common theme I noticed when counseling birth parents who were attempting to reunify with their children was that many of them seemed to recognize the need for healing and expressed a desire for the church and faith to play a role in that. It's no exaggeration when I say that almost 100 percent of the birth parents I counseled in the foster care system inevitably said something along the lines of "I think I need Jesus or the church in my life." *Yes!* And yet, there was resistance. When we explored this further, many parents felt like they couldn't even walk into the church because they would be judged. Hearing stories like these, I began to think, *How would Jesus respond?* I truly believe that if Jesus were walking here on earth, instead of villainizing birth parents, he would show them grace, love, mercy, and most importantly, forgiveness. What a beautiful way we as Christians can model the love of Jesus, by saying, "I'm going to love you, cheer for you, mentor you, and encourage you in this process, regardless of the outcome." Imagine if we as the church had that posture toward our birth parents who were in need of healing?

Additionally, for birth parents who have chosen adoption for their child, this choice can be a deep source of grief, pain, and loneliness. Choosing an adoption plan for one's child inevitably means great loss, even if the decision seems best for everybody. A few decades ago, adoption plans were typically closed: once the child was adopted, no relationship with the birth parents was allowed unless the child was able to track them down after turning eighteen. More and more, open adoption has become the new norm. Open adoption does not meet co-parenting, but some level of contact takes place between the birth parents, adoptive parents, and child. Open adoption plans can take a variety of forms—anything from mailing letters to the birth parent once a year to having an ongoing, interactive relationship including visits, depending on the agreement.

The question you might have after reading this is "How?" How can we practically support and care for birth families in our churches and communities whether they have chosen adoption or are trying to reunify with their children through foster care?

Include Them

Birth parents have received bad press for so long, and adoptive and foster parents have fear and apprehension around them. Granted, in some situations a healthy boundary needs to be in place in regard to a birth parent's choices or behavior, but that is usually the exception, not the rule. To show birth parents love and care, include them in your child's life and your family's life as far as it depends on you. (In some situations, contact with the child's birth parents is not safe or appropriate. For example, if you are a foster family, there may be restrictions on visits.) Invite them to come along when you go to the zoo or take family photos. Make a space for them at the Christmas dinner table. They are a huge part of your child's life. As much as possible, and if they are willing, include them.

Respect Them

Respect goes a long way in caring for and loving birth families. You should always show respect to birth families—first, because they are made in God's image just like you and deserve to be treated with dignity but also because your child is watching and listening. If you respect their birth parents and model that respect for them, they are more likely to grow up with respect not only for their birth parents but all human beings. When I worked in foster care, the birth parents and foster parents sometimes seemed pitted against each other, like it was "us versus them" rather than "us working together" to love and care for the children.

Openly Love Them

To openly love birth parents, take an active interest in all facets of their life. Share in their grief, celebrate in their victories, mourn when they mourn, cry when they cry, and laugh when they laugh. Far too often, we keep love to ourselves. We might feel love for someone but fail to show actions of love. One of the healthiest things you can do for your children is to love their birth parents. I remember counseling a ten-year-old boy who felt angry at his foster parents because he felt like they did not try to help his birth parents get him back. But love is also something you need to do for others, for your own spirit. Choosing to love someone else is food for your heart—not just feeling or thinking love, but living and acting out love. Your child's birth parent already likely carries around the guilt and shame of not being able to be a parent daily. The open love you show for birth parents can help heal these wounds.

Support Them

Sometimes it can feel easier to be uninvolved with the birth family, especially if there is some tension or resentment. The level of support you can engage in can depend on the relationship you have, the adoption plan, or your child's preferences. If this is a foster care situation, you might have limited or no access, but if the adoption is finalized, you have a voice in how much interaction you and your children have with their birth families. My advice: do as much as you can. Find ways to support or be in relationship with them. Offer to help drive them places. Grab a cup of coffee. Pray for them. Be open to serving them. I've seen beautiful friendships develop between birth families and adoptive or foster families. You can show immense love and model it for your child by choosing to support birth parents.

Remember Them

Birth parents have experienced deep loss. Holidays, birthdays, anniversaries, and certain seasons can all be painful moments—or even triggers for birth parents. As best as you can, remember them on these days and encourage them if you have that kind of relationship with them. Send them notes or cards. Be creative.

Treat Them Normally

Birth parents are human beings just like you. Feeling uncomfortable around your child's birth parents is natural, but you need to push past the awkwardness of the situation. They just want to live a normal life like you do. They long for connection to others. If we let the weirdness or awkwardness of a situation dominate our interactions, our children's birth parents will feel as though there is something wrong with them. Even if they have made choices that you consider less than desirable, treat them as you would want to be treated if you were in their shoes.

Honor Your Child's Narrative

Honor your child's narrative by letting your child write or tell her own story about her birth parents. Try as best you can not to influence it. Keeping our opinions from children about their birth parents can be tricky, especially if our viewpoint is negative. We typically have more information than the child does, and yet it's important to let your child formulate his own opinions and beliefs. Children's feelings typically fluctuate over time as they process their experiences. A foster family I was with was navigating these changes. The birth mother was addicted to heroin and was fighting to stay clean. She had left the kids in the care of her boyfriend, who physically abused them. However, despite all these experiences, the eight-year-old girl loved her birth mother deeply and was cheering hard for her to get them back. The foster parents felt so torn: part of them wanted to villainize the birth parent for hurting the children, but villainizing the birth parent would not honor the child's narrative. The children loved their birth parent deeply, and that feeling needed to be honored and validated.

PRACTICAL APPLICATION

In the rest of this chapter, I would like to give an example of what involving the church might look like when caring for vulnerable children. For seven years, I have led a ministry called Replanted, which is designed to provide care and support for adoptive and foster families, and to partner with the local church in this process. When reading about some of the ways Replanted has helped adoptive and foster families, I want to emphasize that this isn't a one-size-fits-all approach. It's more like an example or illustration so that you can get a sense of what support might look like in a church context. If some of these ideas for support resonate with you, great. If not, that's okay too. The point is to show what support and partnership with the local church could look like.

Replanted started in 2011 following a conversation with one of the pastors at my local church. I had been working as a therapist in the foster care system for some time, and I had noticed that the foster and adoptive families on my caseload were having difficulty receiving the support they needed. Many of these families were Christians and involved with the local church. But for many of the reasons I discussed above, they weren't getting the help they needed.

The pastor was adopted himself, and he was passionate about this area of ministry. We were chatting, and he asked, "What do you think it would look like if the church was doing a good job supporting adoptive and foster families? How could we do this better?" This was a great place to start. I had a church partner interested in learning more and invested in helping care for the families who were supporting vulnerable children. There was an openness to get involved—not just to convince families to adopt and foster but to help those families postplacement.

Replanted was never about one individual church—it was about the church as a whole. From the beginning, I realized that my individual church didn't have the resources to support all the adoptive and foster families in the area. Many families attended smaller churches with little or no formal support. A megachurch in my area even struggled to effectively support their adoptive and foster families. For many congregations, it just wasn't a high priority. I quickly realized that if we were going to support the families in need, we were going to have to work together. From the beginning, Replanted involved people from a variety of churches in the area coming together in unity. Your denomination didn't matter. If you were passionate about helping adoptive and foster families, you were welcome at Replanted.

A big learning experience for me came in figuring out the needs in my area. To make this assessment in your particular context, you'd likely need to meet with churches in the area and ask what they are already doing to support adoptive and foster families. If some great things are already happening, don't reinvent the wheel. Your community might also have some other helpful resources, such as foster care agencies. Take stock and see what resources exist so that you can determine the areas where you're needed most.

Have honest conversations with your church about what it can do to support adoptive and foster families in your community. Church members need to do an honest self-assessment: Is this area of ministry for them? What can they realistically provide for adoptive and foster families in terms of money, time, and resources? This learning experience was difficult for me. At times my church would commit to a certain amount of support or money, and then later the budget priorities would change. It can be discouraging to consistently advocate for something when it isn't always supported 100 percent.

After tallying the needs of the adoptive and foster families in my local community, we decided to come up with the three-level approach described in this book of emotional, informational, and tangible support (J. M. Hook et al., 2017). This approach was also supported by research that had surveyed the support needs of adoptive families (Groze, 1996).

For each of those three levels, we started to brainstorm. We also talked with adoptive and foster families in the community to see what they needed and wanted. What were their greatest needs? What would be most helpful right now? What kinds of support were critical? What resources did we have, and how did they fit with the needs? We also let ourselves dream a bit. Like Jesus and the feeding of the five thousand (Matthew 14:13–21), we may have felt like we only had five loaves of bread and two fish, but we trusted God to help meet the needs of our community's adoptive and foster families.

For emotional support, we focused on developing support groups. Our families yearned for connections with other families who empathized and understood. Sometimes our families felt like they were the only ones facing their particular issue, and realizing that they were not alone was so healing for them. The Replanted groups allowed parents and kids to develop supportive relationships with one another, which was perhaps the most critical and successful part of the Replanted ministry. The relationships established enabled families to set up their own sources of support that continued outside of the Replanted ministry.

For informational support, we committed to providing regular trainings on issues that were critical to adoption and foster parenting (such as parenting kids with trauma or attachment issues). We also encouraged our parents to attend conferences and trainings such as Refresh and Empowered to Connect. Families sometimes cannot attend trainings and conferences because of time and cost constraints. The church stepped in and absorbed some of the cost so that parents could gain this critical information that would help their families in the long run.

For tangible support, our goal was to try to get clarity on the most pressing needs of adoptive and foster families and then try to connect the dots and enable the church to meet those needs most efficiently and consistently. For example, new adoptive and foster parents are often stressed out because the transition can be so difficult. We organized a sign-up for families in the church to provide meals to the new family. This activity is ingrained in the culture of most churches for welcoming a biological child, but not so for adoptive and foster families. Don't forget them. We set up a resource closet, where church families could donate needed items such as diapers, food, and clothes for adoptive or foster families who needed them. We set up an adoption fund to help cover some of the costs for families who wanted to adopt but couldn't afford it. Finally, we worked to provide regular respite care for adoptive and foster families. For example, we hosted "Parents' Night Out" events, where adoptive and foster families could drop off their kids and have a date night.

Your own church and community are unique, and the support you provide for adoptive and foster families needs to match individual needs of the people in your immediate area. But the process will likely be similar.

- Take stock and get a sense of the needs of the adoptive and foster families in your community.
- Take an honest look at the resources that you can bring to the table as a church community.
- Try to match your resources to meet the needs that show up in your community.

Your support will likely cover the three key areas we've addressed—emotional, informational, and tangible support—but your context will dictate the specifics for how you can meet the families' needs.

EXERCISE: BECOMING A CHURCH THAT SUPPORTS ADOPTIVE AND FOSTER FAMILIES

Where is your church right now? How involved are you in the lives of adoptive and foster families in your community? What are you doing currently to help support the needs of these families?

_____

_____

_____

_____

_____

How can you support adoptive and foster families before *and* after they take in a child?

_____

_____

_____

_____

_____

How can you and your church become more informed about trauma and other issues that are important when supporting adoptive and foster families?

_____

_____

_____

_____

_____

_____

How can you be humble and listen to the people who are actually involved in the hard work of caring for adoptive and foster families, such as mental health professionals? How can you listen better to the families themselves?

_____

_____

_____

_____

_____

_____

Are you open to partnering with other churches and ministries to set up infrastructure that can meet the needs of adoptive and foster families in your congregation?

_____

_____

_____

_____

_____

_____

How can your church change so that it is characterized by grace, becoming a more welcoming and inviting place for adoptive and foster families who are struggling?

_____

_____

_____

_____

_____

_____

CHAPTER 9

You Are Not Alone

I see the poem or the novel ending with an open door.

—MICHAEL ONDAATJE

I LOVE THIS quote by Michael Ondaatje, and not just because he's Canadian like me. Endings have always been difficult for me. I lived in the same house on the same farm for my entire childhood. (My brother, sister-in-law, and niece now live on the farm, so I get to see it every time I visit them.) Community is very important to me, and I always felt sad when friends would move away, even though I was excited for their next step.

I feel a similar way about ending this book. I care deeply for you and want so badly for you to know that you are loved and not alone. That's the main reason I decided to write this book. In my work, I saw so many adoptive and foster families struggling, with no one to turn to for support. I knew so many families who felt like they were just trying to survive. And let me be clear, I don't just mean in parenting kids from hard places. Raising children who have been impacted by trauma has its own set of hurdles, but adoption and foster care come with many unique journeys that need to be processed. I saw parents struggling with infertility who had entered the adoption or foster care journey without acknowledging or processing their loss and sadness. I saw parents waiting for their much-anticipated adoption to happen, trying to be patient through all the ups and downs. I saw foster parents who thought they would be able to adopt their child and then have to change their plans and expectations when a relative showed up on the scene.

I saw children embarrassed to let others know they were in foster care, like it was a secret that needed to be kept. I saw biological children affected by the trauma of their new sibling and feeling overlooked as their parents needed to give more time and attention to their healing child. This journey is complex. Those of you in the trenches know this firsthand. I thought if I could just connect families with each other, they could know, deep within their souls, that they were not alone—and this desire is just as important for children. Children impacted by adoption or foster care need to be in relationship with each other so that they know, deep in their souls as well, that they are not alone.

Growing up in the church, I also knew that Christians placed a high value on caring for vulnerable children. I would often sit through a sermon and hear the preacher talk about how important it was to care for the orphans and widows. But after the platitudes and the encouraging words often came a disconnect. Even though Christians and churches said they supported adoption and foster care, there was often very little or sometimes zero actual postplacement support. An adoptive or foster parent could go to church, be absolutely drowning, listen to a sermon about how the church should care for vulnerable children, and still receive absolutely no support whatsoever. Something is wrong with this picture—and this problem motivated me to write this book.

Three Key Truths about Caring for Vulnerable Children

Before we end, I want to reiterate some key lessons regarding support for adoptive and foster families. First are three key truths about caring for vulnerable children.

The Work Is Holy

If you are involved in the important work of caring for children through adoption and foster care, I have the utmost appreciation for you and the holy work you are doing. It's the work of the kingdom. I see you and the sacrifices you are making for your kids. I see you up late at night with a crying baby who most of the time can't be consoled. I see you trying to do your best to parent an aggressive child who is acting from his trauma brain. I see you struggling to find time to connect with your spouse amid all the stress and difficulty. I see you grieving because the child you cared for left your home and was reunified with biological parents. You are not alone.

God also sees you. God knows the difficulties you face. God knows that he didn't call you to something easy when he placed one of his precious children in your care. Jesus said that "whatever you did for one of the least of these brothers and sisters of mine, you did for me" (Matthew 25:40). When you slowly rock your child to sleep, when you bandage her knee, when you are patient and gracious with him even though he wet the bed again, you are literally meeting the needs of God himself. Even if the world doesn't notice what you are doing, Jesus notices. You are not alone.

The Work Is Hard

Caring for vulnerable children through adoption and foster care is often challenging. That's reality; the situations leading to both are rarely simple or easy, and the kids have been through it all. Although parents often say that adopting or fostering is one of the things that provides their lives with the greatest sense of meaning and purpose, it is also one of the most difficult and challenging journeys they have ever taken. You are not alone.

Parenting a child with a history of trauma is stressful. When the amygdala kicks in and a child or teen is screaming, hitting, or crying, it takes a toll on you as a parent. It's hard to keep showing up day in and day out when progress seems minimal or nonexistent. It's tough to parent a child who has insecure attachment. You try repeatedly to soothe the child and let him know that he is safe, but something is lost in translation. Even though your precious child knows on some level that he is safe and will have dinner tonight, he's still on guard. The things that he knows in his head don't always translate to the heart and body. You long for your child to snuggle with you and relax as you hold her and stroke her hair, but it rarely happens like you imagined it would. You are not alone.

Then you're dealing with everything else. Your friends and family don't understand what your child or you are going through. They judge and criticize your parenting techniques when they don't have a clue about trauma or attachment. They give advice that you already tried long ago. They stop returning your calls or say that your child isn't welcome on play dates anymore. You are not alone.

Sometimes the system seems to be working more against you than for you. School is tough for your child, and his teachers don't seem to understand. It's challenging to find a good therapist who is trained in trauma and understands your child's particular background and experiences. People make decisions about your child in foster care that are maddening and place her back in a dangerous situation. Sometimes you want to scream and cry and punch someone, because you feel so scared and out of control.

In all the aspects of the kingdom work you do, I see you, God sees you, and you are not alone.

The Work Requires a Team Effort

Caring for children from hard places on your own is tough. You need a support team by your side every step of the way. For much of this book we've discussed what support might look like and how you can get it. First, you need emotional support. You need a group of people around you who extend grace to you and your family. You need people around you who are safe so that you can take off your masks and be vulnerable, even the parts of you that cause you shame. You need people with whom you can be honest, to whom you can tell the truth, and who can tell the truth to you.

Second, you need informational support: information and training so that you can be the best possible parent to your child. You need to understand trauma, trauma-informed parenting, and attachment. The challenges associated with adoptive and foster parenting are significant. We need to be well-informed so that we can draw from a big and varied tool kit when parenting our children.

Finally, you need tangible support. If you don't have your basic needs met, it's tough to do anything well. Think about how to meet your needs for money and supplies so that those issues aren't an additional source of stress. Also think about taking time regularly for self-care. Your kids need parents who are taking care of themselves and who can parent at full capacity.

THREE FINAL THOUGHTS

You may be in the middle of your adoption or foster journey. You might be just getting started, experiencing a mix of hope, excitement, and fear. My own journey in helping support adoptive and foster families is, like parenting itself, a work in progress. I hope to do this work for as long as God enables me to write, speak, and love on precious children and their families.

But our journey together in working through this book is coming to a close. As we part, I'd like to leave you with three final thoughts.

Be Grateful for Your Journey Thus Far

The adoption and foster journey can have many ups and downs. Sometimes it is characterized by struggle and disappointment. Some things may turn out differently than you wanted or expected. You might have made mistakes and carry regrets. And you may have experienced moments of incredible joy that you wished would last forever. You might have memories where you look back and laugh, appreciating God's joy and sense of humor.

Sometimes we have the tendency to feel gratitude for the "good things" in life and regret the "bad things." We label things as "positive" or "negative," not realizing that things are often more complex than that. Some of our biggest lessons can come from mistakes and failures. The times when we struggle the most can also be the times where we feel closest to God. When you look back on your adoption or foster journey thus far, try not to label things as "good" or "bad." Your story isn't finished yet. Your child's story isn't finished yet. You might look back in ten, twenty, or thirty years and see how God was working even in that experience you wish had never happened.

Have Hope for the Future

Nothing is more powerful than hope. And we can have hope because of God's grace and love in our lives. Conversely, nothing is more disheartening and devastating when we lose all hope. Losing hope can feel worse than death. The apostle Paul writes that when all things pass away, three things will remain: faith, hope, and love (1 Corinthians 13:13). Never lose hope. God is always working and always active in your life. His grace is sufficient. The Bible promises us that nothing can separate us from the love of God (Romans 8:38–39).

If you feel like you have lost hope in the future, please reach out to someone for help. Even though I believe with all my heart that nothing can separate us from the love of God, I know that we can certainly feel that way when we are really struggling. Sometimes we need someone to sit with us and be God's presence for us, to put flesh and bones on the promises that we read in scripture. Reach out to your pastor, professional counselor, or a friend. Reach out to me, Josh, or Mike. Reach out to anyone who can remind you of the hope you have in Jesus.

Experience God and Community in the Present

The present can be a difficult time to enjoy because we feel regret and guilt about the past or anxiety about the future—or both. But the present moment is really all we have. The past can't be changed; we can learn from it, but we don't want to stay stuck there. And the future is unwritten; we don't know what will happen in the future, so it's a good idea not to worry too much about it (Matthew 6:34).

The present moment, though, is a gift. In the present we live and make choices that affect our future. In the present we connect and commune with God. In the present we engage with our spouse or friends and do the difficult but awesome work of loving our children. In the present we go to church and ask our community for help and support. The present is where all the magic of living happens, so that's where to focus your energy and attention. Don't miss out on God's gift: your life right now.

BENEDICTION

For you, the adoptive or foster parent, and your family. Receive this prayer of blessing:

> Loving God, your son has taught us that whoever welcomes a child in his name, welcomes him. We give you thanks for this child, whom the parents have welcomed into their family. Bless this family. Confirm a lively sense of your presence with them and grant to these parents patience and wisdom, that their lives may show forth the love of Christ as they bring up their child to love all that is good. We ask this through Christ our Lord. Amen.

EXERCISE: ENDING WELL AND SAYING GOOD-BYE

What are one or two key lessons you gained from reading this book?

_____

_____

_____

_____

_____

_____

Which topic or chapter was most helpful for you?

_____

_____

_____

_____

_____

What is one thing you would like to implement in your life moving forward? What is the first step toward doing so?

_____

_____

_____

_____

_____

_____

_____

Do you have further questions? What are they? Do you know where to go for the information you need?

_____

_____

_____

_____

_____

_____

What is one step you could take to help you get the help and support you need on your adoptive or foster journey?

_____

_____

_____

_____

_____

_____

_____

Is there anything you sense that God is wanting to say to you right now?

_____

_____

_____

_____

_____

_____

Appendix A: Books

GENERAL ADOPTION / FOSTER SUPPORT

Berry, M. (2018). *Confessions of an adoptive parent: Hope and help from the trenches of foster care and adoption.* Eugene, OR: Harvest House Publishers.

Johnson, J. (2018). *Reframing foster care: Filtering your foster parenting journey through the lens of the gospel.* Grand Rapids: Credo House Publishers.

ATTACHMENT

Gray, D. D. (2014). *Attaching through love, hugs, and play: Simple strategies to help build connections with your child.* London: Jessica Kingsley Publishers.

Hoffman, K., Cooper, G., Powell, B., & Benton, C. M. (2017). *Raising a secure child: How Circle of Security Parenting can help you nurture your child's attachment, emotional resilience, and freedom to explore.* New York: Guilford Press.

TRAUMA-INFORMED PARENTING

Purvis, K. B., Cross, D. R., & Sunshine, W. L. (2007). *The connected child: Bring hope and healing to your adopted family.* New York: McGraw-Hill Education.

Schooler, J., Smalley, B. K., & Callahan, T. (2010). *Wounded children, healing homes: How traumatized children impact adoptive and foster families.* Colorado Springs, CO: NavPress.

Siegel, D. J., & Bryson, T. P. (2012). *The whole-brain child: 12 revolutionary strategies to nurture your child's developing mind.* New York: Bantam Books.

SENSORY PROCESSING DIFFICULTIES

Kranowitz, C. S. (2006). *The out-of-sync child: Recognizing and coping with sensory processing disorder.* New York: Skylight Press.

Church Engagement

Johnson, J. (2018). *Everyone can do something: A field guide for strategically rallying your church around the orphaned and vulnerable.* Grand Rapids: Credo House Publishers.

Books for Kids

Kaeb, J. (2018). *Who loves* book series. The Forgotten Initiative.

Lee, C. R. (2015). *It's tough to be gentle: A dragon's tale.* CreateSpace Independent Publishing Platform. (Also check out Cindy Lee's other children's books.)

Wilgocki, J., & Wright, M. K. (2002). *Maybe days: A book for children in foster care.* Washington, DC: APA Books.

Appendix B: Conferences and Retreats

Christian Alliance for Orphans (CAFO) Summit (CAFO.org): Conference offering education and training for adoptive and foster parents, counseling professionals, and church leaders.

Refresh (TheRefreshConference.org, RefreshChicago.net, RefreshKansas.city): Conference offering training, support, and refreshment to adoptive and foster parents.

Rejuvenate Retreat (ForeverHomes.org/Retreats): A retreat for foster and adoptive moms.

Road Trip for Foster and Adoptive Dads (RoadTripDads.com): This retreat experience aims to bring foster and adoptive dads together in community.

Appendix C: Trainings

Trust-Based Relational Intervention (TBRI) (child.tcu.edu): Trauma-informed intervention training that equips professionals to help children heal from trauma.

Empowered to Connect (EmpoweredtoConnect.org): Two-day training based on TBRI principles.

Trauma Competent Care (back2back.org/tcc): A variety of trainings for trauma-informed caregiving.

Appendix D: Websites

FROM THE AUTHORS

Replanted Ministry (ReplantedMinistry.org): Provides postplacement support for adoptive and foster families and engages the local church.

Confessions of an Adoptive Parent (ConfessionsOfAnAdoptiveParent.com): Offers hope and informational support for adoptive and foster parents.

FROM OTHERS

Chosen and Dearly Loved (ChosenAndDearlyLoved.org): Provides support for families adopting children with special needs.

The Forgotten Initiative (TheForgottenInitiative.org): Provides support to foster families.

FosterTheFamilyBlog.com (Jamie C. Finn): Offers hope and encouragement to adoptive and foster families.

JasonJohnsonBlog.com (Jason Johnson): Offers encouragement to adoptive and foster families through his blog and engages the local church.

Lifesong for Orphans (LifesongForOrphans.org): Provides support and funding for adoptive families.

The Out-of-Sync Child (Out-Of-Sync-Child.com): Provides information on sensory processing disorders.

Sensory Processing Difficulties Network (SINetwork.org): Provides information on sensory processing disorders.

Show Hope (ShowHope.org): Provides care for vulnerable children by engaging the church and helping with the adoption process.

References

Ainsworth, M. D. S. (1973). The development of the infant-mother attachment. In B. Cardwell and H. Ricciuti (Eds.), *Review of child development research* (Vol. 3, pp. 1–94). Chicago: University of Chicago Press.

Ainsworth, M. D. S., Blehar, M. C., Waters, E., & Wall, S. (1978). *Patterns of attachment: A psychological study of the strange situation.* Hillsdale, NJ: Erlbaum.

Barna Group. (2013, November 4). *5 things you need to know about adoption.* Retrieved from http://www.barna.com/research/5-things-you-need-to-know-about-adoption

Baumeister, R. F., Bratlavsky, E., Finkenauer, C., & Vohs, K. D. (2001). Bad is stronger than good. *Review of General Psychology, 5,* 323–370.

Bell, R. (2008). *The gods aren't angry.* Grand Rapids: Zondervan.

Bernock, D. (2014). *Emerging with wings: A true story of lies, pain, and the love that heals.* Shelby Township, MI: 4F Media.

Billings, A. G., & Moos, R. H. (1981). The role of coping responses and social resources in attenuating the stress of life events. *Journal of Behavioral Medicine, 4,* 139–157.

Bowlby, J. (1958). The nature of the child's tie to his mother. *International Journal of Psychoanalysis, 39,* 350–371.

Bowlby, J. (1969). *Attachment and loss:* Vol. 1. *Attachment.* New York: Basic Books.

Boyd, G. A. (2004). *Repenting of religion: Turning from judgment to the love of God.* Ada, MI: Baker Books.

Brhel, R. (2009). Dawn of attachment: Why Mom's emotions matter during pregnancy. *The Attached Family.* Retrieved from http://theattachedfamily.com/membersonly/?p=2139

Brown, B. (2017). *Braving the wilderness: The quest for true belonging and the courage to stand alone.* New York: Random House.

Center on the Developing Child at Harvard University. (2017). *Three principles to improve outcomes for children and families*. Retrieved from http://www.developingchild.harvard.edu

Cloud, H., & Townsend, J. (1992). *Boundaries: When to say yes, how to say no to take control of your life*. Grand Rapids: Zondervan.

Davis, D. E., Worthington, E. L., Jr., Hook, J. N., Emmons, R. A., Hill, P. C., Bollinger, R. A., & Van Tongeren, D. R. (2013). Humility and the development and repair of social bonds: Two longitudinal studies. *Self and Identity, 12*, 58–77.

de Shazer, S., Dolan, Y., Korman, H., Trepper, T., McCollum, E., & Berg, I. K. (2007). *More than miracles: The state of the art of solution-focused brief therapy*. Philadelphia: Haworth Press.

Exline, J. J., Pargament, K. I., Grubbs, J. B., & Yali, A. M. (2014). The religious and spiritual struggles scale: Development and initial validation. *Psychology of Religion and Spirituality, 6*, 208–222.

Figley, C. R. (1995). *Compassion fatigue: Coping with secondary traumatic stress disorder in those who treat the traumatized*. New York: Routledge.

Firestone, L. (2012). Are you parenting like your parents? *Psychology Today*. Retrieved from https://www.psychologytoday.com/us/blog/compassion-matters/201211/are-you-parenting-your-parent

Firestone, L. (2015). How your attachment style affects your parenting. *Psychology Today*. Retrieved from https://www.psychologytoday.com/us/blog/compassion-matters/201510/how-your-attachment-style-affects-your-parenting

Gottman, J., & Silver, J. (1999). *The seven principles for making marriage work: A practical guide from the country's foremost relationship expert*. New York: Three Rivers Press.

Groze, V. (1996). *Successful adoptive families: A longitudinal study of special needs adoption*. Westport, CT: Praeger Publishers.

Hoffman, K., Cooper, G., Powell, B., & Benton, C. M. (2017). *Raising a secure child: How Circle of Security Parenting can help you nurture your child's attachment, emotional resilience, and freedom to explore*. New York: Guilford Press.

Holiday, R. (2014). *The obstacle is the way: The timeless art of turning trials into triumphs*. New York: Penguin.

Holmes, T. H., & Rahe, R. H. (1967). The social readjustment rating scale. *Journal of Psychosomatic Research, 11*, 213–218.

Hook, J. M., Hook, J. N., Captari, L. E., Aten, J. D., Davis, D. E., & Van Tongeren, D. R. (2017). Replanted: Offering support for adoptive and foster care families. *Journal of Psychology and Christianity, 36,* 222–229.

Hook, J. N., Davis, D. E., Van Tongeren, D. R., Hill, P. C., Worthington, E. L., Jr., Farrell, J. E., & Dieke, P. (2015). Intellectual humility and forgiveness of religious leaders. *Journal of Positive Psychology, 10,* 499–506.

Hook, J. P., Hook, J. N., & Davis, D. E. (2017). *Helping groups heal: Leading small groups in the process of transformation.* West Conshohocken, PA: Templeton Press.

Hopson, J. L. (1998). Fetal psychology. *Psychology Today.* Retrieved from https://www.psychologytoday.com/us/articles/199809/fetal-psychology

Horvath, A. O., & Greenberg, L. S. (1994). *The working alliance: Theory, research, and practice.* New York: John Wiley & Sons.

James, C. C. (2015). *Half the church: Recapturing God's global vision for women.* Grand Rapids: Zondervan.

Janis, I. L. (1971). Groupthink. *Psychology Today, 5*(6), 43–46.

Johnson, J. (2016, December). Faithfulness, foster care, and trusting God with the rest. *JasonJohnsonBlog.* Retrieved from http://jasonjohnsonblog.com/blog/faithfulness-foster-care

Kranowitz, C. S. (2006). *The out-of-sync child: Recognizing and coping with sensory processing disorder.* New York: Skylight Press.

Lazarus, R. S., & Folkman, S. (1984). *Stress, appraisal, and coping.* New York: Springer.

Lerner, M. (1980). *The belief in a just world: A fundamental delusion.* New York: Plenum.

Lifeway Research. (2018). *Adoption, foster care, commonplace in churches.* Retrieved from https://lifewayresearch.com/2018/01/24/adoption-foster-care-commonplace-in-churches/

Maslow, A. H. (1943). A theory of human motivation. *Psychological Review, 50,* 370–396.

McConnell, M., & Moss, E. (2011). Attachment across the life span: Factors that contribute to stability and change. *Australian Journal of Educational and Developmental Psychology, 11,* 60–77.

McKay, K., Ross, L. E., & Goldberg, A. E. (2010). Adaptation to parenthood during the post-adoption period: A review of the literature. *Adoption Quarterly, 13,* 125–144.

Miller, B. C., & Sollie, D. L. (1980). Normal stresses during the transition to parenthood. *Family Relations, 29*, 459–465.

Moullin, S., Waldfogel, J., & Washbrook, E. (2014). *Baby bonds: Parenting, attachment and a secure base for children.* London: Sutton Trust.

Nickerson, R. S. (1998). Confirmation bias: A ubiquitous phenomenon in many guises. *Review of General Psychology, 2*, 175–220.

Purvis, K. B., Cross, D. R., Dansereau, D. F., & Parris, S. R. (2013). Trust-based relational intervention (TBRI): A systemic approach to complex developmental trauma. *Child Youth Services, 34*, 360–386.

Purvis, K. B., Cross, D. R., & Sunshine, W. L. (2007). *The connected child: Bring hope and healing to your adopted family.* New York: McGraw-Hill Education.

Quiroga, M. G., & Hamilton-Giachritsis, C. (2016). Attachment styles in children living in alternate care: A systematic review of the literature. *Child Youth Care Forum, 45*, 625–653.

Roney, S. (2014, June). *Our adoption story (part 3).* Retrieved from http://www.churchrez.org/news/author/scottroney

Siegel, D. J., & Bryson, T. P. (2012). *The whole-brain child: 12 revolutionary strategies to nurture your child's developing mind.* New York: Bantam Books.

Troutman, B., Ryan, S., & Cardi, M. (2000). The effects of foster care placement on young children's mental health. *Protecting Children, 16*(1), 30–34.

Wetzstein, C. (2012). Study: Families trending toward open adoptions. *The Washington Times.* Retrieved from https://www.washingtontimes.com/news/2012/mar/21/study-families-trending-toward-open-adoptions/

Worthington, E. L., Jr., Davis, D. E., & Hook, J. N. (2017). *Handbook of humility.* New York: Routledge.

Worthington, E. L., Jr., McCullough, M. E., Shortz, J. L., Mindes, E. J., Sandage, S. J., & Chartrand, J. M. (1995). Can couples assessment and feedback improve relationships? Assessment as a brief relationship enhancement procedure. *Journal of Counseling Psychology, 42*, 466–475.

Yalom, I. D. (1970). *The theory and practice of group psychotherapy.* New York: Basic Books.

Index

About the Authors

Jenn Ranter Hook, MA is the founding director of Replanted (www.ReplantedMinistry.org)—a ministry that helps empower the church to support adoptive and foster families. After receiving her master's degree in clinical psychology from Wheaton College, she worked as a therapist for children in the foster care system. She is a trauma-specialized therapist and a Trust-Based Relational Intervention (TBRI) practitioner. She speaks frequently on topics related to adoption and foster care support, mental health, and trauma. She lives in Dallas, TX with her husband Josh.

Joshua N. Hook, PhD, is an associate professor of counseling psychology at the University of North Texas and is a licensed clinical psychologist (LCP). He has written four books, including *Helping Groups Heal: Leading Small Groups in the Process of Transformation* (Templeton Press, 2017). He blogs regularly about psychology and faith at www.JoshuaNHook.com. He lives in Dallas, TX with his wife Jenn.

Mike Berry is an author, podcaster, speaker, and parent coach. He and his wife Kristin are parents to eight children, all through adoption, and served as foster parents for eight years. Mike has written four books, including *Winning the Heart of Your Child: 9 Keys to Building a Positive Lifelong Relationship with Your Kids* (Baker Publishing Group, 2019). He is also the cocreator, along with Kristin, of the award-winning blog www.confessionsofanadoptiveparent.com. He lives on a farm with his family just outside of Indianapolis, Indiana.

CONNECT WITH REPLANTED AT

https://replantedministry.org/

[f] @Replanted Ministry

[o] @Replanted Ministry

[t] @replantedmin